The Lincoln Image

The Lincoln Image

ABRAHAM LINCOLN AND THE POPULAR PRINT

HAROLD HOLZER

GABOR S. BORITT

MARK E. NEELY Jr.

University of Illinois Press

Urbana and Chicago

∞ This book is printed on acid-free paper.

Library of Congress Cataloging-in-Publication Data
Holzer, Harold.
The Lincoln image : Abraham Lincoln and the popular print /
Harold Holzer, Gabor S. Borritt, Mark E. Neely, Jr.
p. cm.
Originally published: New York : Scribner Press, c1984.
Based on an exhibit of engravings and lithographs at
Gettysburg College.
Includes bibliographical references and index.
ISBN 0-252-02669-1 (cloth : alk. paper)
1. Lincoln, Abraham, 1809–1865—Pictorial works—
Exhibitions. 2. Presidents—United States—Pictorial works—
Exhibitions. I. Boritt, G. S., 1940– . II. Neely, Mark E. III. Title.
E457.65.H64   2001
973.7'092—dc21   00-053278

University of Illinois Press
1325 South Oak Street
Champaign, IL 61820–6903
www.press.uillinois.edu

For my parents,
for Edith,
and for Remy and Meg

      —H.H.

For my father's eightieth birthday,
to the memory of my mother,
and to their grandchildren,
Norse, Jake, and Daniel

      —G.S.B.

Contents

Correction to Photo Credits

In 1992 the Louis A. Warren Lincoln Library and Museum changed its name to The Lincoln Museum. All pictures credited to the Louis A. Warren Lincoln Library and Museum are in the collection of The Lincoln Museum, with the following reference numbers: p. XVII: TLM #2834; p. 12: TLM #2024/2665/3419; p. 21: TLM #0-2; p. 25: TLM #2805; p. 26: TLM #0-17; p. 29: TLM #2483; p. 30: TLM #2055; p. 35: TLM #2214; RFA p. 36: TLM #3356; p. 39: TLM #431; p. 41: TLM #419/2660; p. 48: TLM #2367; p. 55: TLM #1931; p. 58: TLM #0-9; p. 60: TLM #2349; p. 68: TLM #197; p. 72: TLM #394; p. 76: TLM #1987; p. 77: TLM #1988; p. 85: TLM #2297; p. 92: TLM #2304; p. 97: TLM #2313; p. 98: TLM #0-92; p. 100: TLM #2643; p. 101: TLM #200; p. 103: TLM #2793/2794; p. 105: TLM #2051; p. 112: TLM #2832; p. 119: TLM #0-97; p. 129: TLM #3252; p. 130: TLM #441; p. 131: TLM #3884; p. 133: TLM #2622; p. 135: TLM #0-88; p. 137: TLM #2804; p. 138: TLM #1990; p. 141: TLM #0-91; p. 142: TLM #2422A; p. 143: TLM #2313/2470; p. 144: TLM #3295; p. 150: TLM #1713/2803; p. 151: TLM #2800; p. 152: TLM #2258; p. 155: TLM #1420; p. 157: TLM #1691/2583; p. 163: TLM #2209; p. 170: TLM #0-93; p. 173: TLM #2777; p. 75: TLM #2211; p. 177: TLM #148; p. 178: TLM #2250; p. 185: TLM #2786/2865; p. 186: TLM #926; p. 189: TLM #2210; p. 192: TLM #XXX; p. 195: TLM #3452; p. 196: TLM #3324; p. 201: TLM #3282; p. 207: TLM #312; p. 210: TLM #2812; p. 213: TLM #2856.

Preface to the Illinois Edition

We began writing this book eighteen years ago to accompany an exhibition of engravings and lithographs that opened at Gettysburg College in 1984 and later ran at the Fort Wayne Art Museum, the Lincoln Boyhood Home in Indiana, the John Hay Library at Brown University, and other venues across the country.

Jacques Barzun took the book to the publishing house of Charles Scribner, and Maron Waxman, assigned as our editor, came up with the title *The Lincoln Image* and shepherded the project into print.

But then Scribner's was unexpectedly absorbed by Macmillan, and offices and warehouses were moved and moved again. By the time the cloth-bound edition was sold out and the time seemed right for a paperback, the publishers could no longer locate the original plates.

The development of new printing technologies has at last made possible a reprint of this study of old printing technologies. Plates and film are no longer needed to facilitate republication, not even for lavishly illustrated volumes such this one. We are greatly indebted to Willis G. Regier, director of the University of Illinois Press, for engineering this new edition of *The Lincoln Image*.

When we first wrote the book in 1984, we declared: "We are making a beginning." Since that time, other scholars have produced fine studies on collective public memory and political culture, many of which have included the area of iconography—as we hoped. The field is engaging new readers, and we trust that they will continue to find our work useful.

HAROLD HOLZER
GABOR S. BORITT
MARK E. NEELY JR.
October 2000

Acknowledgments

We are grateful to Gettysburg College, the host of the exhibit of engravings and lithographs on which this book is based. We wish to acknowledge the enthusiastic support of President Charles E. Glassick; Dean David B. Potts; Vice President Richard P. Allen and his staff; James Agard, the curator of the Gettysburg College Art Gallery; and the members of the department of history; Basil L. Crapster, chairman, Bruce W. Bugbee, George H. Fick, Norman O. Forness, Charles H. Glatfelter, and J. Roger Stemen.

We wish to thank the Lincoln National Life Insurance Company of Fort Wayne, Indiana, especially its chief executive officer, Ian M. Rolland, for generous support for our work. David Allen, senior vice president, gave crucial moral support.

Support came also from the Pennsylvania Humanities Council, its executive director, Craig R. Eisendrath, and its assistant director, Carol Coren. We must also note the help of the Pennsylvania Council on the Arts and its executive director, June Batten Arey, and the director of its Crafts and Visual Arts/Museums Programs, Richard E. Siegesmund.

Our consultants on the exhibit have been Richard N. Current, Don E. Fehrenbacher, Lillian B. Miller, Wendy Wick Reaves, and Milton Kaplan. Samuel A. Streit, head of the John Hay Library at Brown University, offered welcome encouragement.

Among the many individual scholars and students whose advice was sought and absorbed over the years are three pioneers in Lincoln picture research: Stefan Lorant of Lenox, Massachusetts, Lloyd Ostendorf of Dayton, Ohio, and R. Gerald McMurtry of Fort Wayne, Indiana. Frank J. Williams, president of the Lincoln Group of Boston, provided support. James T. Hickey, curator of the Illinois State Historical Library in Springfield, Illinois, threw open the print and document files of his institution. Bernard Reilly of the Library of Congress did the same. Stanley King and William Kaland, two important New York collectors, gave freely of their advice and ideas. And encouragement came from Richard Sloan, president of the Lincoln Group of New York, and George M. Craig, of the Civil War Round Table of New York.

Elaine Hirschl Ellis graciously permitted us the first publication of Thomas Johnston's painting of Lincoln, and her father, Norman Hirschl, proprietor of the Hirschl & Adler Galleries in New York, made available his archival notes on the long-lost picture. Joseph L. Eisendrath generously made available the previously unknown portrait of Thomas Doney. Ray Reynolds of San Diego, California, shared his research materials on the American Bank Note Company's Lincoln print, and Stanley J. Richmond of the Daniel F. Kelleher Galleries of Boston supplied the photograph. Maxwell Whiteman, curator of the art collection of the Union League of Philadelphia, provided information on and photographs of E. D. Marchant's painting of Lincoln. J. Rufus Fears and Ruth Bavlantos shared their classical learning with us. William F. Hanna pointed out a period comparison between Lincoln and John Brown. Charles H. Glatfelter called our attention to the Bikle manuscript.

At Scribners, we are much indebted to Jacques Barzun, for his early interest in and enthusiasm for this book, and to our editor, Maron L. Waxman, whose incisiveness and breathtaking speed never ceased to amaze us. A special salute goes to Jewel Fowler, who typed and retyped the manuscript, and to Sandra Jones, who served as the central repository for messages both between the authors and with the publisher.

Finally, we owe thanks to those in our families whose patience and good will exceeded our best hopes, even as our demands on them surely surpassed their worst fears. Sylvia Neely not only read the manuscript but checked and rechecked the footnotes. Edith Holzer read and reread the drafts of the text. And the various members of the Holzer and Boritt households—Remy and Meg in the former, and Liz, Norse, Jake, and Daniel in the latter—endured months during which there were few subjects of conversation at the breakfast and dinner table except Abraham Lincoln.

By the People, For the People

The President last night had a dream.

He was in a party of plain people and as it became known who he was they began to comment on his appearance. One of them said, "He is a very common looking man." The President replied, "Common looking people are the best in the world: that is the reason the Lord makes so many of them."

Waking, he remembered it, and told it as rather a neat thing.

Diary entry by John Hay,
Lincoln's private secretary,
December 24, 1863.[1]

Gettysburg, Pennsylvania, November 19, 1863. Dedication day for the Soldiers' National Cemetery on the site of the most famous battle of the Civil War:

AT the northwestern corner of town, the students of Pennsylvania College, now Gettysburg College, prepared to march in the procession toward the cemetery, hurrying to join the parade assembling at the town square. There, the military units lined up first, then the civil divisions, with the students close to the very end. One of the students, sophomore Philip M. Bikle, would long remember the college boys' chagrin at their "inconspicuous position of tailenders."[2] Nonetheless, they had resolved to march along the well-decorated route, where flags were draped in mourning on that sunny Indian summer day. Like the thousands of visitors who thronged the town that morning, they were eager to get a glimpse of the President of the United States. Abraham Lincoln had come to deliver a brief address at the dedication ceremonies.

They had their first chance to see Lincoln when he emerged onto the square from the Wills House, where he had spent the night. Dressed in his customary black Prince Albert coat, a wide silk mourning ribbon circling his stovepipe hat, Lincoln stood tall in the vast crowd, waiting patiently for the parade to get under way. Finally, after a long delay, the procession started, with the students bringing up the rear. At the cemetery, however, a pleasant surprise awaited them. The column divided, and the tail-

H. B. Hall, *Diogenes His Lantern Needs No More,/ An Honest Man Is Found!— The Search Is O'er*. Published by N. P. Beers, New York (1865). Engraving, 12⅛ × 15¾ in. Lincoln's fabled honesty was at the core of a public image that endures to this day. Lincoln owed his election to the presidency in 1860 in no small part to this image, summed up in the political sobriquet invented for the campaign: "Honest Abe, the Railsplitter of the West." It connoted integrity and, implicitly, the American dream of the right to rise. By 1865, the year of his assassination, the Lincoln image had grown richer. Now he was also the Great Emancipator, the savior of the Union and the martyr of liberty. This post-assassination rendition of the search of the ancient Greek philosopher for an honest man indicates that Lincoln's integrity continued at the heart of what Americans saw in him. The image thus survived the painful, testing years of tenure in office, essentially because it was based on reality. (*Louis A. Warren Lincoln Library and Museum*)

enders were allowed "to march through and halt directly in front of the large platform built for the speakers and other dignitaries."[3] Lincoln now sat a few feet away, waiting his turn to address the large audience.

Until that day, these students—most of the people in the crowd—had never seen the President. Yet they all recognized him. *Carte-de-visite* photographs, woodcuts in the nationally distributed New York illustrated newspapers, and print portraits purchased at print shops, bookstores, and newspaper offices, through the mails, or from itinerant agents, had turned the unknown face of a Western politician into the best-known face in the United States in a brief period of time. Prints, in particular, had not only helped make Lincoln familiar but also palatable, romanticizing his homeliness and glorifying his accomplishments. They had traced his emergence as a dark horse, backwoods presidential candidate and his transformation into a bearded statesman, the Emancipator. Remembering some of these pictures while standing on the field still dotted with battle mementos, the students and the rest of the audience at Gettysburg were able to compare the original model with their expectations of his appearance.

From the Gettysburg of 1863 the path leads to the Gettysburg of 1984, a town whose name is now immutably tied to Lincoln's. Here an exhibit of engravings and lithographs was created to commemorate the 175th anniversary of Lincoln's birth: "The Lincoln Image: Abraham Lincoln and the Popular Print." The exhibit, at Bikle's alma mater, Gettysburg College, assembled not only the best and rarest but also some of the worst and most common Lincoln prints in an attempt to recover their meaning

ABRAHAM LINCOLN.

DIOGENES HIS LANTERN NEEDS NO MORE,
AN HONEST MAN IS FOUND THE SEARCH IS O'ER.

for Lincoln's America. Out of that exhibit came this book, the first to explain how a primitive industry shaped its unappreciative subjects for a passionately political audience.

Lincoln and other public men of his era were not particularly image-conscious because their age was not as image-saturated as ours. Television, film, lavishly illustrated magazines, and photojournalism bombard us with pictures of instant celebrities and depict newsworthy events for mass consumption on the very day they occur. During the Civil War, existing technology did not permit newspapers to reproduce on their pages the few photographs available to them, all of which were static or posed. Weeks elapsed before even a portrait of a person in the headlines could appear in shop windows or in the few illustrated periodicals. It is enormously difficult for us to imagine a time when pictorial images were rare and precious rather than contemptibly common and routinely manipulated. The crudeness of many Lincoln engravings and lithographs reminds us that Americans in those days did not get to see many pictures. The distinct craftsmanship in other prints, in turn, reveals the time and effort that necessarily intervened between the people and the pictures of their political heroes.

Politics rather than baseball or football was then the national sport, and politicians really were heroes, more often dubbed with such loving nicknames as Gallant Harry of the West or Father Abraham than with the belittling ones of today, like Tricky Dick. A desire existed to know what these heroic men looked like—far exceeding what is often mere curiosity in the modern era—and an industry peculiar to the nineteenth century grew to meet it: the commercial publication and distribution of lithographs and engravings of political figures. Using photographs or, more rarely, paintings as models, commercial lithographers and engravers produced single-sheet political prints that, from all indications, hung in homes just as reproductions of landscapes or celebrity posters do today.

The presence of political images in the home, perhaps the most sacred of Victorian institutions, as well as in the marketplace, demands more attention than it has received to date. The fate of the popular prints so much in evidence in public places and private homes during Lincoln's day instead has been to vanish from view, almost totally hidden today in map cases and storage vaults in research libraries and museums. They are stepchildren in the former, where books and documents are the premier attractions to scholars. And they are poor relations in the latter, lacking the prestige, originality, and—it must be admitted—artistic merit of fine paintings. Not surprisingly, then, large collections of Lincoln prints have rarely been displayed. The first such exhibition, at New York City's Grolier Club, did not occur until thirty-four years after Lincoln's death. The eighty-five years since that landmark exhibition have seen few similar exhibits, no exhibit catalogues, and only one book, an unfinished attempt simply to make a list of Lincoln prints without interpretation or research into their uses.[4] For too long the prints have remained virtually unexplored intellectual territory.

The 1984 Gettysburg exhibit opened up that territory. (The exhibit traveled first to New England, to Brown University's John Hay Library, then to the West, to the new Fort Wayne Museum of Art.) This book explores it further—within specific boundaries. The exhibit and the book are limited to separately published prints, among them cartoons and illustrated sheet music, and with one exception exclude book, magazine, and newspaper illustrations.

The Lincoln Image includes not only pictures of the Lincoln photographs and paintings from which prints were derived, but other materials that help explain the relationship between Lincoln's image, the printmakers' craft, and the political culture which helped shape both of them. The focus is on the prints produced in Lincoln's lifetime and in the iconographically important months immediately following his death. The last two engravings in the book, which date from 1866 and 1869, are included because they point toward the best of what was to come in Lincoln prints after the heroic age in which his image was forged. They are landmarks of the next era, which would see Lincoln transfigured into an American icon, rigid but symbolizing the enduring ideals of the nation itself.

This is by no means a collection of all Lincoln prints published through 1865. Their number is far too great and our ability to identify them too limited (many were undated and lacked printmaker credits). Besides, the results of such an accumulation would be terribly repetitious. We believe that what survives is representative of what there once was, and this book contains a broad sample of the surviving prints.

Like all political evidence, prints must be used with care. They were no more "accurate" than stump speeches, newspaper editorials, or party platforms, but they have some of the same ability as those more familiar sources to reveal the hopes and fears of Americans in the nineteenth century. Like all documents, they may be revealing without being truthful. We have tried always to keep in mind the distortions of commerce, with its often careless haste to meet market demands and its anxiety to please and to avoid impropriety.

As political image-shapers, printed pictures complemented the printed word. Historians of the Lincoln era have long studied the words. It is time to study the pictures, too. We are making a beginning.

PART I

"Introducing a Rail Old Western Gentleman"

Tell us of his fight with Douglas—
  How his spirit never quails;
Tell us of his manly bearing,
  Of his skill in splitting rails.

Tell us he's a second Webster,
  Or, if better, Henry Clay;
That he's full of genial humor—
  Placid as a summer's day.

Call him Abe, or call him Abram—
  Abraham—'tis all the same,
Abe will smell as sweet as either,
  We don't care about the name.

Say he's capable and honest,
  Loves his country's good alone;
Never drank a drop of whiskey—
  Wouldn't know it from a stone.

Tell again about the cord wood,
  Seven cords or more per day;
How each night he seeks his closet,
  There, alone, to kneel and pray[.]

Tell us he resembles Jackson,
  Save he wears a larger boot,
And is broader 'cross the shoulders,
  And is taller by a foot.

Any lie you tell we'll swallow—
  Swallow any kind of mixture;
But oh! don't, we beg and pray you—
  Don't, for God's sake, show his picture.

—"LINCOLN'S PICTURE,"[1]
Democratic campaign song, 1860

I T REQUIRES a considerable leap of historical imagination to appreciate the pictures of Abraham Lincoln that were offered the American public in defiance of that Democratic wish. The precise analogue of the political prints of the Civil War era hardly exists today. Americans have lost their taste for them.

To be sure, there are political images aplenty on the contemporary scene. But they do not show up in the same places that nineteenth-century political prints did. No one today would expect to find framed portraits of Ronald Reagan or Jimmy Carter anywhere save at party headquarters or in public buildings—least of all in private homes. Few people not officially connected with the Defense or State Department would care to own a picture of the heads of those departments, much less to display them on the walls of their den. Nor would one expect to open a family's photograph album and find, before moving on to snapshots of the baby's christening and the Fourth of July picnic, a picture of the President of the United States, portraits of his cabinet members, or even a picture of John Hinckley, who attempted to assassinate President Reagan.

In Lincoln's era, however, the print industry and the fledgling photograph industry supplied political pictures that were used in precisely those ways by Americans of all classes. Fifty-cent lithographs and ten-dollar steel engravings had different sorts of purchasers, but the most remarkable fact to us today is that they did have customers—in the thousands. Hundreds of Victorian parlor albums survive, their cardboard pages holding *carte-de-visite* photographs of statesmen and politicians at the start and trailing off into unidentifiable portraits of the owner's family toward the end. Even political cartoons, many of those from Lincoln's era published as individual prints or "poster cartoons" rather than in periodicals, apparently found substantial audiences, no matter how savage or ephemeral their theme.

A political environment peculiar to the nineteenth century sustained the market for political prints. Two features distinguished that environment from the political environment today: first, the sheer importance of politics in daily life; and second, its thoroughly partisan nature.

In the absence of organized sports and anything but the most rudimentary entertainment industry, politics, with its hours of dazzling oratory, campaign songs, torchlit parades, fireworks, banners, badges, posters, and prints, offered spectacle, ritual, and time-filling amusements to an America of island communities locked in rural isolation. It was as though football and the process of choosing leaders had been combined into a single emotion-filled phenomenon. Americans "go to great mass meetings," a *Harper's Weekly* editor observed in 1860, "during the pleasant summer months of a campaign, as they go to theatres and other places of amusement during the winter, to be entertained . . . . Banners, torches, music, rallying cries, symbols of every kind increase the good-humored excitement." When Lincoln met Stephen A. Douglas in Ottawa, Illinois, in the first of their famous debates in 1858, the little town with its population of six thousand was thronged with ten thousand people. "There was a vast concourse of people," Lincoln reported afterward to a political associate, "—more than could [get] near enough to hear." Many, of course, came simply for the spectacle.[2]

In an age with no motion pictures or television and few illustrated periodicals, spectacle was an important drawing card, and Abraham Lincoln's first campaign for the presidency, in 1860, employed spectacle in a big way, much bigger than usual.

"Hurrah" campaigns (or "hullabaloo" campaigns, as some political scientists call them) were a relatively recent phenomenon, forever associated in old Whigs' minds with their first national party success, the election of William Henry Harrison in the landmark log cabin and hard cider campaign of 1840.

Lincoln was an old Whig himself, a veteran of that 1840 campaign, and he was leading a new political party in 1860, the majority of whose members were also former Whigs. Yet he had not always been comfortable with hurrah campaigns. In 1840, while Harrison remained so silent on the issues that Democrats called him "General Mum," Lincoln gave complicated speeches on national banking. Whig setbacks, especially in overwhelmingly Democratic Illinois, gradually wore Lincoln's principles down. By 1848, when the Whigs were running another bland general, Zachary Taylor, in an opportunistic campaign, Lincoln had better adapted himself to the hurrah techniques. He instructed his law partner:

> You young men get together and form a Rough & Ready club, and have regular meetings and speeches. Take in every body that you can get . . . but as you go along, gather up all the shrewd wild boys about town, whether just of age, or a little under age. . . . Let every one play the part he can play best—some speak, some sing, and all hollow. Your meetings will be of evenings; the older men, and the women will go hear you; so that it will not only contribute to the election of "Old Zach" but will be an interesting pastime, and improving to the intellectual faculties of all engaged.

By 1860 Lincoln was at the very least willing to sit by quietly and let the Republicans "all hollow."

Lincoln's "Railsplitter" image, created at the Illinois Republican convention in 1860 when enthusiastic supporters hauled in two old fence rails, the kind Lincoln had split thirty years before, immediately conjured up memories of the Harrison log cabin campaign. This was noted at the time, for example by the Democratic organ in Cleveland:

> The Republicans are endeavoring to strengthen a weak nomination by some of the stale electioneering tricks borrowed from former campaigns. Every one recollects how, in the time of Harrison, the log cabin and hard cider dodge was worked throughout the country. . . .
>
> Having cast aside a candidate [William H. Seward] who, but for treachery, might have been run on his own personal merits, the Republicans have resorted to the device of investing their present choice with imaginary antecedents, which they think have a chance of appealing to the popular heart.

The Democrats were right in a way. After John C. Frémont's loss of the presidential election in 1856, the Republicans, as one historian has put it, "became less issue oriented and more winning oriented."[3]

Soon after Lincoln's nomination, Republicans introduced the "Wide Awakes," groups of young men usually dressed in black oilcloth capes and caps, who carried "rails" with torches on them in spectacular nighttime parades for Lincoln—"forests of torches," said one correspondent who witnessed a huge parade in New York City. Some units wore red capes and hats for variety, and some carried blue or red oil lamps. They "had the appearance of a Chinese Feast of Lanterns." Large floats on flatbed wagons pulled by six- and eight-horse teams dotted the parades. Glee clubs practiced campaign songs for weeks. Steampresses on floats turned out campaign poems before the onlookers' very eyes. Even humble parades were punctuated with Roman candles; larger parades boasted rockets. All of them featured mottoes on painted banners and ended in speeches, speeches, speeches.[4]

There was more emotion invested in all this than in any ordinary amusement because, after all, it was also a part of choosing the government. Some travelers to the United States sensed the greater solemnity of purpose in the spectacle. Michel Chevalier, a French visitor, noted in 1839 the striking resemblance between Democratic political parades and the religious processions he had seen in Mexico and Europe: torches, mottoes, "magic lantern" transparencies, and halting places. Little wonder, then, that Robert Philippe, in the section of his *Political Graphics: Art as a Weapon* dealing with the prints of Lincoln's era, says: "One of the functions of political prints has always been to decorate the walls of people's houses. In this sense they are the heirs of the sacred picture. They testify to convictions, and provide reassurance of ways of being."[5]

There is less willingness today to "testify" to political convictions by hanging pictures of party heroes in private homes. If there was any similar desire to keep one's party affiliation private in the nineteenth century, it was to no avail. The peculiar political institutions of that day demanded a public display of partisanship.

There was no secret ballot. Every time Abraham Lincoln won election before becoming President, he won it by receiving oral votes. Illinois did not abolish *viva voce* voting until 1848, so citizens of that state had to proclaim their convictions out loud in public if they wanted to vote at all. The paper ballots that eventually replaced oral voting offered little improvement in the way of privacy, for the parties, not the government, printed the ballots. Typically, they printed them in different colors. Usually, a voter took his colored ballot from a temporary booth identified by party and dropped it into one of two clear bowls, identified by party posters, inside the polling place.

Political "independence" was unknown. Fewer than 5 percent of the voters switched party from election to election in the 1840s. Almost every voter identified with a party. If his party ran a candidate he did not like, he stayed home; switching to the other party was all but unthinkable.

Like individual voters, newspapers were closely identified with party. There was no independent press and no ideal of journalistic independence. Almost all newspapers were funded by a party, either directly or indirectly (by the party's dragooning its adherents into subscribing to the paper). Thus the newspaper one bought, quoted, and carried under one's arm was as sure a public sign of partisan identification as the color and placement of one's ballot. Voter turnout was enormous—almost 80 percent nationally in 1840. Nearly everyone was accustomed to having his partisanship known in public. It is no wonder that in this atmosphere in which politics were important and no one feared showing his political convictions, political prints thrived as decorations even in private homes or businesses.

Although partisanship was a basic assumption of political behavior in the nineteenth century, the unwritten rules for presidential candidates harked back to the eighteenth century, when parties were considered evil and there was no real concept of a legitimate opposition. Presidential candidates were not supposed to campaign. Lincoln chose not to, but Stephen Douglas, his northern Democratic rival, became the first presidential nominee ever to do so. The degree to which a presidential candidate could properly encourage campaigning on his own behalf was uncertain, and the uncertainty extended to the arrangements for providing pictures of himself. Asked for a photograph only two short months before the Republican National Convention, Lincoln responded: "I have not a single one now at my control; but I think you can easily get one at New York. While I was there I was taken to one of the places where they get up such things, and I suppose they got my shaddow, and can multiply copies indefinitely. Any of the Republican Club men there can show you the place."[6] The "shaddow" sounds like a bit of folksy posturing, but the letter proves that Lincoln at that time had no photographs of his own to distribute publicly and no definite arrangement with a supplier.

The unwritten rules governing the behavior of presidential candidates seemed to render even an appearance at the nominating convention too much like a show of lust for office. With barely four weeks remaining before the start of the Republican National Convention of 1860, Abraham Lincoln had still not decided whether to travel to Chicago for the great event. Responding to a Chicago banker who offered to open his home to Lincoln if he chose to attend (hotel reservations in the city were already growing scarce), Lincoln would only say: "Whether I shall be able to attend the Chicago convention, I have not yet determined."[7] The date was April 14. The Republicans were set to convene in thirty-two days, and still Lincoln could not make up his mind.

His reluctance to commit himself to appearing on the scene was not meant to convey indifference over the proceedings themselves. There was no question, in fact, but that Abraham Lincoln had been incurably bitten by the presidential bug. "The taste *is* in my mouth a little," he would admit in an "entirely frank" letter to a long-time supporter. Yet he still felt it his duty to pledge that under no circumstances would he permit his "pretensions" to reach "the point of endangering our common cause," the election of the nation's first Republican chief executive.[8]

Lincoln was a dark horse candidate, and he knew it. His only hope of winning the nomination was to become everybody's second choice, the candidate to whom delegates could most comfortably turn in the event the pre-convention favorites stumbled. "I have not heard that any one makes any positive objection to me," Lincoln noted, and that was good. "Our policy then," he instructed one follower, "is to give no offence to others—leave them in a mood to come to us, if they shall be compelled to give up their first love."[9]

Lincoln's personal role in this plan was a difficult one. He would have to give the impression of availability while suppressing the appearance of eagerness. Besides, Lincoln professed to believe that "when not a very great man begins to be mentioned for a very great position, his head is very likely to be a little turned."[10] Ultimately, he chose to stay in Springfield while his political fate was being decided in Chicago.

Nevertheless, Lincoln's "head" proved to be very much in evidence in the Wigwam, the temporary "small edition of the New York Crystal Palace" built expressly for the Republican convention in Chicago. There were woodcut portraits in the picture newspapers from the East, likenesses on display in the hallways of the Wigwam, and, most important, a specially printed bundle of pictures ready to be used by his supporters in the pro-Lincoln floor demonstrations later in the week.

In an atmosphere clouded by cocktails before breakfast, one journalist, Murat Halstead, noted that the "badges of different candidates are making their appearance, and a good many of the dunces of the occasion go about duly labeled. I saw an old man this morning with a wood-cut of Edward Bates pasted outside his hat. The Seward men have badges of silk with his likeness and name, and some wag pinned one of them to Horace Greeley's back yesterday, and he created even an unusual sensation as he hitched about with the Seward mark upon him."[11] What may well have been the most sensational pictorial display of all, however, was yet to come. One historian later called it "the shower of Lincoln prints at the Wigwam"[12]—a confetti-like outpouring of Lincoln images released, evidence suggests, at the moment his name was formally offered to the convention for the presidency.

As one contemporary described the scene: "The crowded audience greeted this nomination with perfectly deafening applause, the shouts swelling into a perfect roar, and being continued for several minutes, the wildest excitement and enthusiasm prevailing."[13] Lincoln's supporters, jamming the balconies in disproportionate numbers thanks to counterfeit admission tickets, capped the demonstration by letting loose their arsenal of pictures, hand-colored wood engravings by E. H. Brown (Fig. 1). The first print portrait of Abraham Lincoln had "found" its market.

On one of the very few surviving copies, George William Curtis, editor of *Harper's Weekly,* inscribed in pencil: "These prints were showered through the Wigwam immediately after Mr. Lincoln's nomination May 1860."[14] Curtis, serving as a delegate to the convention, no doubt caught one of the copies as it floated down from the mezzanine. Another editor-delegate, Horace Greeley of the *New York Tribune,* brought his copy of the print back to his newspaper offices the following week. "While he was

STATE SOVEREIGNTY. NATIONAL UNION.

Copyright Secured.

ABRAHAM LINCOLN.

FROM A PHOTOGRAPH BY HESLER.

relating some of the stirring incidents of that memorable day," a witness recalled, "he took, from the side pocket of his coat, a wood-cut which appeared like a caricature of a very plain man, and holding it up, that all might see it, he said, with an air of triumph: 'There, I say, that is a good head to go before the people'; and we all agreed that it was." The witness judged that "This picture had been made quickly, when Mr. Lincoln's chances for the nomination became probable, and was roughly done. . . ."[15]

The absence of anything in the caption indicating the candidate's political aspirations has stimulated the belief among some historians that Lincoln's campaign organization at Chicago was until the very last moment prepared to settle for the vice-presidential nomination—in which case this catchall print would still have served some purpose.[16] Another explanation is that a suggestion of specific ambition might have been construed by the delegates as one of those "pretensions" against which Lincoln had taken such great care to caution his supporters. Thus the Wigwam print did not say: "Our Choice for President," but merely: "Abraham Lincoln," along with the Illinois state motto: "State Sovereignty [and] National Union."

The convention, "wildly excited," nominated Abraham Lincoln for President on the third ballot, amid "cheering, shouting and waving hats." What followed, in the absence of the nominee himself for the now-obligatory appearance before his party, was yet another parade of Lincoln portraiture. "The first roar of the cannon soon mingled itself with the cheers of the people," reported the *New York Times,* "and at the same moment a man appeared in the hall bringing a large painting of Mr. LINCOLN." A

FIGURE 1. E. H. Brown, *Abraham Lincoln/From A Photograph by Hesler,* Chicago (1860). Woodcut engraving, 6 × 8 in. The first known separate-sheet print portrait of Lincoln, this crudely executed image, based on an 1857 photograph (Fig. 2), was issued for the Republican National Convention in 1860. A newspaper advertisement (see Fig. 13) offering for sale a subsequent edition of this print later that summer boasted of its "beautiful emblematic Border . . . denoting strength and victory," and quoted a critic's view that the Lincoln portrait featured "a spiritual expression, such as his countenance assumes when he is engaged in debate." (*Louis A. Warren Lincoln Library and Museum*)

bit later on, "amidst renewed cheers," came "a life-size portrait of ABRAM LINCOLN . . . exhibited from the platform." Another observer remembered it as "a photograph of Abe Lincoln which had hung in one of the side rooms . . . held up before the surging and screaming masses."[17] Of these convention pictures, only the E. H. Brown woodcut is known.

To one correspondent, "the scene" was almost beyond description: "11,000 inside and 20,000 or 30,000 outside . . . yelling and shouting at once." But were they shouting *for* the display of portraits—or in spite of it? There is some evidence to suggest that the portraits may not have achieved their desired effect. One of the witnesses to the scene, Montgomery Blair, later to become Lincoln's postmaster general, thought that the display had actually had an unsettling effect on the convention. He told an artist some years later that "there was a hideous painting in the hall which was brought forward . . . as a likeness of the nominee. Most of the delegates having never seen the original, the effect upon them was indescribable."[18]

As for E. H. Brown's Wigwam print of Lincoln, it was "circulated" throughout the city of Chicago after the convention adjourned.[19] But as Greeley had observed, the picture was crude, and the other Lincoln images at the convention were cruder. Something more accurate and more artistic would be required for other cities curious about the little-known candidate's looks.

Nothing less could be expected of America's printmakers, despite the immaturity of their techniques. In Lincoln, they were given artistically and commercially stimulating raw material: an all-but-unknown face, which the nation would soon be clamoring to see. The opportunities for complementing such presentations with allegorical and biographical accompaniment would arise as well. Here, personified in the rugged physiognomy and self-made personal history, were the basic inspirations for a popular campaign the likes of which had not been played out in American politics since the log cabin contest twenty years before.

Lincoln had been described from the floor of the convention as the "young giant of the West" and "the man who can split rails and maul Democrats," the "youngster who, with ragged trousers, used barefoot to drive his father's oxen and spend his days in splitting rails . . . risen to high eminence." Mr. Lincoln "is a man of the people," gushed the Chicago *Press and Tribune* on the eve of the balloting for president. "All his early life a laborer in the field, in the saw-mill, as a boatman . . . as a farmer . . . he has that sympathy with the men who toil *and vote* that will make him strong. . . . Himself an outgrowth of free institutions, he would die in the effort to preserve to others, unimpaired, the inestimable blessings by which he has been made a man."[20]

The Democratic press did not like doing battle against the American dream. "We do not deny to Mr. Lincoln the merit of having made good use of his opportunities and means," said the Philadelphia *Evening Journal,*

> and we should like to see him enjoy all the just rewards of his manly industry and self-reliance and self improvement. But . . . [i]t does not by any means follow that because an individual who, beginning life as a flat-boatman and wood-chopper, raises himself to the position of a respectable County Court lawyer and a ready stump speaker, is therefore qualified to be President of the United States . . . it will not do to say that he is qualified . . . because, as a boy, he split logs and steered a "broadhorn" on the Mississippi.

Said another paper: "Let us put these [rails] entirely out of the account, and judge Mr. Lincoln solely by his intellectual and political record as a public man."[21]

There were two notable differences from the 1840 campaign in the use of all this log cabin imagery. First, Lincoln really had been born in a log cabin in frontier poverty (unlike Harrison, a Virginia aristocrat). Second, and more important, the success of the economics of the American dream was itself a critique of Southern society, and pointing to Lincoln as a symbol of that success fit the sectional essence of the new Republican party. Greeley's *Tribune* put it very well:

> [Lincoln] is Republicanism embodied and exemplified. Born in the very humblest White stratum of society, reared in poverty, earning his own livelihood from a tender age by the rudest and least recompensed labor . . . his life is an invincible attestation of the superiority of a Free Society, as his election will be its crowning triumph. That he split rails is of itself nothing; that a man who at twenty was splitting rails for a bare living is at fifty the chosen head of the greatest and most intelligent party in the land, soon to be the Head also of the Nation—this is much, is everything.[22]

Early in the campaign an Illinois paper advertised "a spirited Engraving printed in four colors, representing 'OLD ABE, THE RAILSPLITTER,' at his work MAULING RAILS. Flatboat on the left, Steamboat, Farm House and Landscape in the distance, Ox team hauling Rails, etc. In the fore-ground is ABE, Splitting Rails (good likeness), dinner basket, dog, and a copy of 'Blackstone's Law Commentaries' . . . this is a document every Republican should have in his possession." The prints sold for 25 cents each, $8 a hundred.[23] The print here described, like many others, is lost to us, but its message and its motive remain clear a century after publication.

These were the prints that took obvious advantage of Lincoln's personal history. Other artists relied on straightforward portraiture to introduce the little known Lincoln to his new national constituency. For these craftsmen there would be a problem—one which they could and would help overcome themselves—and that was Lincoln's unconventional appearance.

In the words of journalist Donn Piatt, expressed long after "the multiplicity of photographs and engravings" had made his face "familiar to the public," Lincoln "was the homeliest man I ever saw." Echoed the candidate's long-time law partner, William H. Herndon, who wrote lengthy descriptions of Lincoln's features without ever quite conveying what his colleague looked like: he was "not a pretty man by any means, nor was he an ugly one; he was a homely man, careless of his looks, plain-looking and plain-acting." A print salesman in Fond du Lac, Wisconsin, would despair as election day approached and he had sold just one Lincoln lithograph. He explained, "The *face,* say the ladies, is so *homely; so mortally homely.* This, after all, is the great difficulty. Ladies, you know, *rule* in such matters. What they *like,* their husbands, quite generally, will buy. But *what lady likes a homely face?* Not one! Hence, when I have shown the lithograph to my lady friends . . . the cry has uniformly been: 'Why, what an ugly face; I hope, in all conscience, Lincoln does not look like that!'"

When *Harper's Weekly* published a woodcut portrait of the new candidate on the cover of one post-convention edition, postal workers in at least one Southern city refused to distribute copies. After the editors of the Charleston *Mercury* saw the *Harper's* engraving, they commented in print on the portrait, describing Lincoln as "a lank-sided Yankee of the unloveliest and of the dirtiest complexion." To the *Mercury*, this early print portrayed a "horrid looking wretch . . . sooty and scoundrely in aspect, a cross between a nutmeg dealer, the horse-swapper, and the night man, a creature fit evidently for petty treasons, small stratagems and all sorts of spoils." Even to his northern foes, Lincoln's looks seemed alarming. Boston's pro-Douglas newspaper, the Boston *Herald*, pointed out that Lincoln's features were thin and spare, "reminding one very much of Ossawottamie [John] Brown, of Harper's Ferry notoriety."[24]

From the outset of the campaign, Lincoln's appearance seemed to spark controversy and, among his supporters, concern. Wrote John Locke Scripps in the Chicago *Tribune*: "Ten thousand inquiries will be made as to the looks, the habits, tastes and other characteristics of Honest Abe. . . . Always clean, he is never fashionable; he is careless but not slovenly. . . . A slightly Roman nose, a widecut mouth and a dark complexion, with the appearance of having been weatherbeaten, completes the description."[25] This passage was considered flattering enough at the time to qualify for republication as part of a campaign pamphlet. Lincoln himself read and approved it before its reproduction.

As in the debate over the relative merit and relevance of Lincoln's early life of manual labor, the candidate had his defenders. Henry Villard of the New York *Herald*, for example, complained: "I do not understand why Mr. Lincoln is represented as being so prodigiously ugly." He added: "I have never seen a picture of him that does anything like justice to the original."[26]

The challenge was evident. Most people did not know what Lincoln looked like, but they had heard that he was ugly. The printmakers were specially equipped to handle the Republicans' problem. Print portraits could parlay the advantages of serious life portraiture (color and dramatic license) and the photograph (reproducible at modest cost), while minimizing the disadvantages of each: for paintings, their limited audience potential, and for photographs, their static, studio-bound artistic vision.

There was no doubt that it would also be in the best interests of the printmakers themselves to make Abraham Lincoln a prime subject for artistic attention in 1860. It was not merely because Lincoln was not well known or that his public craved his picture; it was also that 1860 was emerging as a watershed year for the printmaking industry, marked by the introduction of rival pictorial processes. Engravers and lithographers could ill afford to leave Lincoln to their competitors.

In 1860, the *carte-de-visite* photograph made its American debut. These visiting card-size images could be mass-produced and sold in multiple copies in numbers which earlier photographic processes—the daguerreotype and the ambrotype, for example—had failed to achieve and with a clarity of line and tone the more recent ferrotype process could never equal.[27] Until then, printmakers had blithely copied one-of-a-kind daguerreotypes, as Philadelphia engraver John Sartain had done for his *Union Magazine of Literature and Art*.[28] To Sartain and others, the medium of photography had long provided inspiration, not competition. Now photographic reproductions would be proliferating along with print portraits. Prints would still monopolize the market for larger scenes, but the *carte* threatened engravers and lithographers with the first real challenge to their dominance of the national audience for popular portraiture.

There were even those, like art critic Coleman Sellers, who

argued that the print industry had all but outlived its allure. "The engraving or etching claimed among the 'modern fine arts,' " he wrote, "is not the work of an artist, it is the work of a printer, who may be a very uneducated man with no artistic taste." Photography, he argued, deserved far greater praise.[29] That printmakers, in the wake of these threatening developments, managed to retain their grip on the pulse of American artistic taste, calculating the marketplace and not only surviving but thriving in the decades to come, is a tribute to their ingenuity and resourcefulness.

To one concerned Republican party official, prints might provide the answer to a simple but vexing problem: "There are thousands . . . who do not yet know Abraham Lincoln." To others this meant encouraging the proliferation of such pictures, even as Lincoln, in keeping with the unwritten rules of decorum for presidential candidates, "held his tongue" and "calmly awaited the result." And by all means, the pictures should be flattering. As the artist Francis B. Carpenter knew, "The effect of such influences, though silent, is powerful. Fremont once said to me that the villainous wood-cut published by the 'New York Tribune' the next day after his nomination, lost him twenty-five votes in one township, to his certain knowledge."[30]

In their rush to produce these eagerly awaited print portraits, most engravers and lithographers quickly copied and restyled existing photographs; a few prepared new and altogether original work. Unfortunately, the latter proved the exception, not the rule. The majority of publishers preferred to hurry less imaginative work to the market. They set a precedent for speed, not style, that dictated the manner in which most print portraitists would continue to depict Lincoln for the remainder of his life.

The initial prints of Lincoln the presidential candidate were

modeled after photographs, some of them new, but others dating back as far as the 1857 camera study by Alexander Hesler (Fig. 2), upon which the crude Wigwam engraving had also been based. Eastern printmakers—for example, Currier & Ives in New York City and E. B. & E. C. Kellogg in Hartford, two of the most prolific—had easier access to an Eastern photograph, Mathew Brady's February 1860 study of Lincoln (Fig. 6) as he appeared on the day of his decisive Cooper Institute Address, a pose which Brady believed was "the means of his election."[31] West of the Hudson River, from Buffalo all the way to Illinois, printmakers seemed attracted to or better able to obtain the Western-looking Hesler photograph, a fact that could not have much pleased Lincoln's image-conscious strategists but seems to have provided a good deal of amusement to the candidate himself.

FIGURE 2. Photograph by Alexander Hesler, Chicago (February 28, 1857). *(Louis A. Warren Lincoln Library and Museum)*

Engraved and Published by T. Doney, Elgin, Ill.
W. Pate, 16 Burling Slip, N.Y.

Yours truly
A. Lincoln.

FIGURE 3. Thomas Doney, *Yours truly/A. Lincoln* [facsimile signature], Elgin, Illinois, and New York City (copublished there by W[illiam]. Pate) (1860). Mezzotint engraving, 19 ⁹⁄₁₆ × 26 ½ in. The most romanticized of the campaign-inspired reworkings of the 1857 Hesler photograph (Fig. 2), Doney's interpretation transformed Lincoln's wild republican hair into a more stylish coiffure. To achieve this effect, Doney simply darkened the background, camouflaging the stray locks that had been so visible in the photograph. (*Library of Congress*)

The Wigwam engraving had been based on the Hesler photograph, and an Elgin, Illinois, engraver named Thomas Doney made a later adaptation of it (Fig. 3). Doney sent a copy of his print to the candidate. If he was hoping for a ringing endorsement from Lincoln, he would be disappointed. The candidate's "indifferent" reaction, delayed until he was reminded to write it, seemed perfectly to exemplify the ambivalence typical of Lincoln on the subject of his portraits. He generally cooperated with those who suggested that his likeness be captured, but he seemed unable to understand why such a fuss would be made about any candidate's appearance, especially his.

> Springfield, Ills.
> July 30, 1860
>
> Thomas Doney, Esq.
> My dear Sir:
> The picture (I know not the artistic designation) was duly and thankfully received. I consider it a very excellent one; though, truth to say, I am a very indifferent judge.
>
> The receipt of it should have been acknowledged long ago; but it had passed from mind until reminded of it by the letter of our friend, Dr. Dodson. Yours very truly
>
> A. LINCOLN[32]

Perhaps his letter to Doney reflected Lincoln's struggle to maintain the proper balance between his personal diffidence and his political ambition: the picture of Lincoln the candidate was "excellent," but Lincoln the man was "indifferent." Perhaps, too, his enigmatic response also reflected Lincoln's ignorance of art— "My judgement is worth nothing in these matters," he admitted.[33]

FIGURE 4. Thomas Doney, French-born engraver. Doney had been a printmaker for more than fifteen years when he produced his 1860 Lincoln mezzotint (Fig. 3). Early in his career he had engraved for Godey's *Lady's Book*. Like most printmakers, he was nonpartisan when it came to publishing pictures. In the 1840s he produced engravings for the *American Whig Review* (see Frank Weitenkampf, *American Graphic Art*, New York: Henry Holt, 1912, pp. 117–118), and around the same time advertised "Portraits of Eminent Democrats," $6 for 50 copies, $10 for 100 (files in the print collection of the New York Public Library). He finished his career in the late 1870s as a photographer. (*Joseph L. Eisendrath*)

By focusing on electoral success rather than issues, the campaign abounded, as one historian has noted, in portrayals "of Lincoln as a human being, a man of the people in whom ordinary Americans could take pride and with whom they could identify. A key ingredient in this endeavor was the promotion of Lincoln's nickname 'Old Honest Abe' or its variants. . . . This sobriquet served Lincoln well, establishing his identity in millions of minds as a down-to-earth, homespun pillar of personal integrity." The printmakers' contribution to this perception "dovetailed nicely with Lincoln's desire to wage a cautious campaign that would alienate as few voters as possible."[34]

"There is enough of romance and poetry in his life to fill all the land with shouting and song," wrote the Chicago *Press and Tribune*. About a dozen lithographed sheet music covers (see Fig. 14), for Lincoln grand marches, Lincoln polkas, and Lincoln Schottisches—patriotic and ethnic rhythms to appeal to various voting blocs—exemplified in exuberance and optimism the glorification of this common man with common music. In one example of campaign sheet music (Fig. 5), decorated with a cover portrait based on Hesler's Western photograph, lyricist D. Wentworth wrote a campaign appeal characteristic of 1860:

Our foe is divided and rent, boys—
They're going to ruin quite fast,
Let them down on their knees and repent, boys,
And "own up" the "nigger" at last.

Then we'll up with our banners and shout, boys,
And the principle boldly contest,
And the foe we will gallantly rout, boys,
With Honest Old Abe of the West.

FIGURE 5. J. Sage & Sons, *Honest Old Abe/Song & Chorus/Words by/D. Wentworth, Esq./Music by/A Wide Awake.* [with facsimile signature: *Yours truly/A. Lincoln.*], published by Blodgett & Bradford, Buffalo, New York (1860). Two-color lithographed sheet music cover, 9 ¾ × 14 in. (oval portrait 5 × 6 in.). Presidential campaign songsters and sheet music began appearing during the election of 1800 and proliferated during such "hullabaloo" campaigns as the Harrison election of 1840 and the Lincoln race of 1860. This particular effort emphasized a central theme of the 1860 Republican campaign: Lincoln's integrity. The portrait for the cover was based on the 1857 Hesler photograph (Fig. 2), with the image reversed, possibly as a means of making the pose seem fresh and original, or of disguising its origins so that the printmaker could avoid paying royalties to the photographer. (*Louis A. Warren Lincoln Library and Museum*)

HONEST OLD ABE

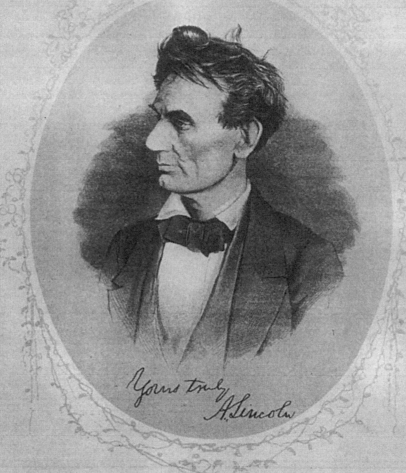

SONG & CHORUS
WORDS BY
D. WENTWORTH, ESQ.
Music by
A WIDE AWAKE.

Published by BLODGETT & BRADFORD 209 Main St.
BUFFALO, N.Y.

J. Sage & Sons, Buffalo, N.Y.

Entered according to Act of Congress AD 1860 by Blodgett & Bradford in the Clerks Office of the Dist. Court of the Northern Dist. of New York.

Then, hurrah! hurrah! hurrah! . . .
For Honest Old Abe of the West;
He will wind up the race in a hurry
And distance their bravest and best.

Along with the hurrahs, of course, could come the avoidance of any expression of sympathy for the black man. The free soil ideology of the Republicans could combine hatred of slavery with a measure of racism.[35]

In addition to sheet music cover likenesses, there were separate-sheet portraits for home display, illustrated broadsides for posting on fences, walls, and tree trunks, and engraved and lithographed cartoons, probably issued for distribution to the party faithful from the offices of the partisan newspapers.

The firm headed by Nathaniel Currier and James Merritt Ives (Fig. 7) was the most prolific of all print publishers of the period, with several thousand titles already to their credit. Their "pictures for the people" were more important than those of most of their rivals because they enjoyed wider distribution through a network of mail order, street, and shop sales. The firm boasted in a sales letter to its dealers: "Our experience of over thirty years in the Trade enables us to select for Publication, subjects best adapted to suit the popular taste, and to meet the wants of all sections, and our Prints have become a staple article which are in great demand in every part of the country."[36]

One expert on Currier & Ives prints claimed that Lincoln "was made to order for the house of Currier, which made the most of him."[37] The quotation surely refers to the Lincoln of 1865 and after, the national myth and martyr. In 1860, the firm treated him no differently than it had been treating presidential nominees for

FIGURE 6. Photograph by Mathew Brady's studio, New York City (February 27, 1860). Taken the day Lincoln delivered his Cooper Institute address, the pose has come to be known as the "Cooper Institute" photograph. *(Louis A. Warren Lincoln Library and Museum)*

FIGURE 7. Nathaniel Currier and James Merritt Ives. *(Museum of the City of New York)*

FIGURE 8. Currier & Ives, *Hon. Abraham Lincoln./"Our Next President,"* New York (1860). Hand-colored lithograph, 9 1/4 × 13 1/8 in. Based on an 1858 photograph, probably by Roderick M. Cole of Peoria, Illinois, this print—despite the implications of its caption—was not issued after Lincoln won the 1860 presidential election, but before. It was a campaign portrait; Currier & Ives issued a similar "Our Next President" lithograph for John Bell, the candidate with the least chance of winning the four-way race. *(Louis A. Warren Lincoln Library and Museum)*

years, as the subject of a series of by then fairly standard prints put out for all candidates in a presidential election year. Altogether, they produced seven portraits of Lincoln in 1860. For his three opponents they produced, respectively, five of Douglas, five of John C. Breckinridge, and four of John Bell.[38]

The disparities in number seem easy to explain. Lincoln was widely thought to be a shoo-in because of the split in the Democratic party. Thus good business sense might have dictated betting the most prints on the winner. Of at least equal importance, Lincoln was the dark horse candidate whose face was unknown to the voters; there was surely the greatest curiosity about his looks. Bell had little chance of winning—hence the scarcity of his portraits. Currier & Ives offered the same number of new portraits for Breckinridge as for Douglas.

Of course, the number of separate poses says nothing about the quantities of any individual portrait printed. Such information appears to be unobtainable. Moreover, Currier & Ives seems not to have been terribly systematic. Printing "Our Next President" below a candidate's name, for example, meant nothing in particular. In 1860 this was done for a Lincoln portrait (Fig. 8) as well as a Bell portrait but not for Douglas or Breckinridge.

A. Lincoln.

HON. ABRAHAM LINCOLN.

"OUR NEXT PRESIDENT"

Currier & Ives responded to the demand for Lincoln images with a series of portraits (see Fig. 9) based on Brady's Cooper Institute photograph. The only print of himself autographed by Lincoln (Fig. 10) was also based on this photograph. Several of Currier & Ives's Eastern rivals also copied the photograph, occasionally disguising their lack of originality by reversing their adaptations into mirror images, in which Lincoln's recognizable facial mole would invariably appear on the wrong cheek. These early images lightened Lincoln's swarthy complexion and, in general, were meant to soften the rough lines of his countenance.

Concurrently, Currier & Ives published more than a dozen different political cartoons (see Figs. 16–19) in which Lincoln figured prominently. These separate-sheet lithographs constituted another part of the print business. Most authorities agree that

ABRAHAM LINCOLN

AMERICAN BANK NOTE CO.

A. Lincoln

FIGURE 10. [A. Sealy], *Abraham Lincoln*, published by the American Bank Note Company (January 1861). Engraving, 6 × 9 in. (portrait approx. 2 × 2 in.). The only print portrait Lincoln is known to have autographed, this engraving is one of three known copies he apparently signed en route to his inauguration as President. According to surviving records of the American Bank Note Company, six proof copies were sent to Lincoln in Springfield shortly before he left for Washington, possibly for his approval. Evidently Lincoln took the proofs with him on his inaugural journey. On February 18, 1861, the inaugural train stopped in Buffalo, New York, where, it was claimed, Lincoln presented one copy to William M. Kasson, the man who had designed the special railroad car in which the President-elect was traveling. According to a testimonial written some seventy-five years later by the designer's son: "My father was . . . introduced to Mr. Lincoln, who warmly thanked him. . . . Upon the termination of that interview, Mr. Lincoln reached down and into his carpetbag, took out a small engraved likeness, which, he remarked, was his favorite picture of himself, and gave it to my father, after having autographed it with the stub of a lead pencil,—as you see, 'A. Lincoln.'" (Typescripts by Mahlon O. Kasson and H. Victor Keane, Illinois State Historical Library.) Another copy, sold at auction in 1965, bears this inscription on the back: "This portrait was presented to me in February 1861 during the journey to Washington, previous to his inauguration. The signature is genuine. J. R. Drake." (*Charles Hamilton Galleries Auction No. 6*, January 14, 1965, p. 32.) A third autographed copy surfaced in 1976 and was sold to a private collector. Perhaps Lincoln never signed another print because the paper used for many engravings and lithographs did not take ink well; signatures smeared or bled, and even artists' proofs were signed in pencil. This may be the reason that Lincoln signed all three known copies of this engraving in lead pencil. The portrait was based on the February 1860 Brady photograph (Fig. 6). (*Daniel Kelleher Galleries*)

FIGURE 11. Photograph by Samuel M. Fassett, Chicago (October 4, 1859). (*Chicago Historical Society*)

FIGURE 12. Edward Mendel [*Abraham Lincoln*], Chicago (1860). Lithograph, 24 × 28 in. This campaign print was based on the Fassett photograph (Fig. 11); printmaker Mendel added the props (a table, a bust of Washington, and a copy of the 1860 Republican platform). He also romanticized Lincoln's features. The mouth was altered, the cavernous hollows of the eyes lightened, the hair tinted and sculpted, and Lincoln's tie straightened; the back of his chair was even extended, so he would not appear quite so tall in the lithograph. When this print portrait was published, its distributors advertised it as the "Largest . . . yet Published" and one which Lincoln himself had pronounced true to life (see Fig. 13). It sold at the time for 75 cents, or $6 per dozen. A copy of Mendel's print framed in pieces of rail split by Lincoln hung on a flagstaff in the yard of the residence of the editor of Springfield's Republican newspaper as the focus of a political rally in August 1860. (C. Jackson to Robert Todd Lincoln, April 24, 1886, Robert Todd Lincoln Letterbooks, Illinois State Historical Library.) (*Chicago Historical Society*)

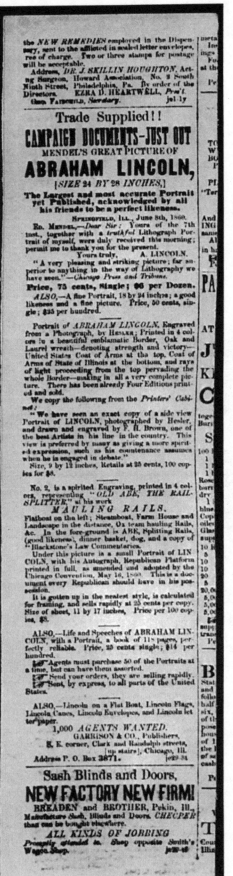

Trade Supplied!!

CAMPAIGN DOCUMENTS—JUST OUT

MENDEL'S GREAT PICTURE OF

ABRAHAM LINCOLN,

[*SIZE 24 BY 28 INCHES,*]

The Largest and most accurate Portrait yet Published, acknowledged by all his friends to be a perfect likeness.

SPRINGFIELD, ILL., June 8th, 1860.

ED. MENDEL,—*Dear Sir ;* Yours of the 7th inst., together with a *truthful* Lithograph Portrait of myself, were duly received this morning; permit me to thank you for the present.
Yours truly, A. LINCOLN.

"A very pleasing and striking picture; far superior to anything in the way of Lithography we have seen."—*Chicago Press and Tribune.*

Price, 75 cents, Single ; $6 per Dozen.

ALSO,—A fine Portrait, 18 by 24 inches; a good likeness and a fine picture. Price, 50 cents, single ; $25 per hundred.

Portrait of *ABRAHAM LINCOLN*, Engraved from a Photograph, by HESLER; Printed in 4 colors in a beautiful emblematic Border, Oak and Laurel wreath—denoting strength and victory—United States Coat of Arms at the top, Coat of Arms of State of Illinois at the bottom, and rays of light proceeding from the top pervading the whole Border—making in all a very complete picture. There has been already Four Editions printed and sold.

We copy the following from the *Printers' Cabinet :*

"We have seen an exact copy of a side view Portrait of LINCOLN, photographed by Hesler, and drawn and engraved by F. H. Brown, one of the best Artists in his line in the country. This view is preferred by many as giving a more spirited expression, such as his countenance assumes when he is engaged in debate."

Size, 9 by 12 inches, Retails at 25 cents, 100 copies for $8.

No. 2, is a spirited Engraving, printed in 4 colors, representing "*OLD ABE, THE RAIL-SPLITTER*" at his work

MAULING RAILS.

Flatboat on the left; Steamboat, Farm House and Landscape in the distance, Ox team hauling Rails, &c. In the fore-ground is ABE, Splitting Rails, (good likeness), dinner basket, dog, and a copy of "Blackstone's Law Commentaries.

Under this picture is a small Portrait of LINCOLN, with his Autograph, Republican Platform printed in full, as amended and adopted by the Chicago Convention, May 16, 1860. This is a document every Republican should have in his possession.

It is gotten up in the neatest style, is calculated for framing, and sells rapidly at 25 cents per copy. Size of sheet, 11 by 17 inches, Price per 100 copies, $8.

ALSO,—Life and Speeches of ABRAHAM LINCOLN, with a Portrait, a book of 118 pages, perfectly reliable. Price, 25 cents single ; $14 per hundred.

☞ Agents must purchase 50 of the Portraits at a time, but can have them assorted.

☞ Send your orders, they are selling rapidly.

☞ Sent, by express, to all parts of the United States.

ALSO,—Lincoln on a Flat Boat, Lincoln Flags, Lincoln Canes, Lincoln Envelopes, and Lincoln letter paper.

1,000 *AGENTS WANTED.*

GARRISON & CO., Publishers,
S. E. corner, Clark and Randolph streets, [up stairs], Chicago, Ill.
Address P. O. Box 3871. je29-34

Sash Blinds and Doors.

NEW FACTORY NEW FIRM!

BREADEN and BROTHER, Pekin, Ill., Manufacture Sash, Blinds and Doors. CHEEPER than can be bought elsewhere.

ALL KINDS OF JOBBING

Promptly attended to. Shop opposite Smith's Wagon Shop. je29-46

FIGURE 13. An enlargement of an advertisement that appeared in the *Tazewell County Republican* of Pekin, Illinois, on July 13, 1860. Among the campaign documents "just out" was "Mendel's Great Picture of Abraham Lincoln," which, its distributors proclaimed, had been "acknowledged by all his friends to be a perfect likeness." To bolster their claims, they reprinted a letter from Lincoln to Mendel thanking him for a gift of what he termed "a *truthful* Lithograph Portrait of myself." More than a century later, the original letter was discovered in Florida, still treasured by Mendel's descendants. (*Illinois State Historical Library*)

---

they must have been sold not only to individuals but also in bulk to party headquarters, particularly since some of them were printed in quantities of 50,000 and 100,000.[39] They were sold at newspaper offices, the nineteenth-century equivalent of party headquarters.

There were other cartoon publishers besides Currier & Ives (see Fig. 20), but none, Currier & Ives included, has received much praise from critics. In fact, the American cartoons of the Civil War have taken a universal critical drubbing. Histories of that art seem so eager to move on to Thomas Nast and the era of the illustrated weeklies that they give the products of the Civil War little attention. One writer attributes American backwardness in caricature to a lack of emphasis on drawing in the school system. Two others say that the era's cartoonists failed to understand the power of cartoons drawn in series to play on one theme. Still others fault the cartoonists for a lack of "moral earnestness," and Currier & Ives in particular for producing work "which makes us wonder whether the artists evolved the idea themselves, or had it given them . . . by the lithographic firm." The same writers fault some for "intemperate partisanship" as well. The most recent book similarly finds the era's caricatures "spiritless," "the product of several hands," and sometimes too much given to "special pleading." The original *Vanity Fair* magazine, a periodical published in New York from 1859 to 1863, thus failed in part (it is said) because its cartoons "were too anti-Lincoln and anti-Negro for a nation engaged in a Civil War over slavery." Even the most sympathetic critic, William Murrell, blamed the lack of any continuous journalistic medium for keeping American graphic humor in its infancy.[40]

The fact of the matter is that modern taste much prefers the

FIGURE 14. T[homas]. S. Sinclair, *Lincoln Quick Step./Dedicated to the/Hon. Abraham Lincoln*, published by Lee & Walker, Philadelphia, and H. M. Higgins, Chicago (1860). Colored lithographed sheet music cover, 9 ½ × 12 ¼ in. The portrait of Lincoln is based on the 1859 Fassett photograph (Fig. 11), but the music cover offered a good deal more: representations of Lincoln as railsplitter (top) and flatboatman (bottom), as well as a border design decorated with the tools of each of those trades. Many lithographers began their careers doing such work for music publishers. As early as 1851, a critic had praised Sinclair for demonstrating "a skill . . . which it is doubtful . . . the best French artists" could surpass. (Marzio, *The Democratic Art*, p. 32.) (*Louis A. Warren Lincoln Library and Museum*)

FIGURE 15. W[illiam]. H. Rease, *The Union Must and Shall Be Preserved*, Philadelphia (1860), published by Rease. Lithograph, 16 ¾ × 11 ⅜ in. Lincoln (his portrait is based on the Fassett photograph, Fig. 11) is here portrayed alongside his running mate, Hannibal Hamlin, in a campaign print rich in political symbolism. A blacksmith and a woodsman jointly guard a shield bearing the motto: "Protection to American Industry." In the distance loom the masts and sails of a ship and the smokestacks of an industrial plant. The message is clear: the Republicans are the party of the American dream, bustling commerce, opportunity, and prosperity—the opposite of the world the slaveholders made. The slogan at top, "Free Speech. Free Homes. Free Territory," printed on a drape slung over a Lincolnesque rail fence, broadens the party's 1856 campaign cry with an allusion to the new homestead plank in the party platform. "Protection to American Industry" was a key message in tariff-mad Pennsylvania. Rease, the printmaker, was considered "American's favorite trade card artist" at the time. (Wainwright, *Philadelphia in the Romantic Age of Lithography*, p. 78.) (*Louis A. Warren Lincoln Library and Museum*)

simple caricature with its clever exaggeration of feature to the typically crowded, wordy, and near-photographic lithographed poster cartoons of the Civil War. Because they are not much admired, they are not much studied or understood. None of the reasons cited for the poor state of the art in that period seems compelling. The status of drawing in American education surely did not change much between the Civil War and the Gilded Age. There was opportunity well before Nast's era to draw cartoons in series in the illustrated weeklies in New York City (*Harper's Weekly* and *Frank Leslie's Illustrated Newspaper*), and Currier & Ives alone

FIGURE 16. Currier & Ives, *"The Nigger" in the Woodpile*, New York (1860). Lithograph (probably by Louis Maurer), 12 × 11 ⅞ in. Currier & Ives published not only bland and celebratory portraiture, but a body of sometimes savage lithographed cartoon posters. More were anti-Lincoln than not. Lincoln here attempts to delude "Young America" into believing no "Negro Problem" exists by concealing a symbolic slave within the planks of the "Republican Platform," a woodpile constructed from Lincoln-split rails. Horace Greeley, who appeared regularly in anti-Lincoln caricature, tries to reinforce the party's posture, but "Young America" replies, "You can't pull that wool over my eyes, for I can see 'the Nigger' peeping through the rails." The reference to "wool" was a pun on the widely used racist term for a black person's hair. The portrait of Lincoln was based in part on the Hesler photograph taken in 1857 (Fig. 2). *(Harry T. Peters Collection, Museum of the City of New York)*

"THE NIGGER" IN THE WOODPILE.

published enough cartoons in the 1860 campaign to permit some concentration on constant themes or symbols.

Indeed, Louis Maurer (1832–1932) and other Currier & Ives artists did just that, using Lincoln's rail as a vehicle on which the candidate could ride, as a baseball bat, and as a platform "plank," among other things. One cartoon of the period, *Introducing a Rail Old Western Gentleman,* depicted Lincoln as nothing more substantial than a scarecrow, literally strung together from his familiar log rails.

These cartoons retained the rather static look of the age. They were made worse because popular ignorance of the candidates' faces forced the artists to eschew caricature and copy photographs, perching the posed heads on bodies made to do other things than pose. Nonetheless, they frequently attained a compelling visual simplicity. What might be termed the "essential" anti-Lincoln cartoon of 1860, *The Rail Candidate* (Fig. 18), combined Lincoln and his ubiquitous rail with the eccentric reformer Horace Greeley (himself a moon-faced walking caricature, with a funny rim of whiskers and a long white duster filled with polemical publications) and the almost universally despised Negro. A stroke of cruel genius turned the Negro into P. T. Barnum's "freak" pygmy, the "What Is It?", his likeness lifted from an advertisement in another Currier & Ives cartoon (Fig. 17).

Maurer's cartoons formed a series, of a sort, in which language balloons and pictorial clutter were kept to a minimum. The principal problem with these pictures is that modern Americans do not care for their social content, a revolting reminder of the aggressively racist common denominator of public opinion in Lincoln's day. And this is to some degree symptomatic of one powerful underlying cause for the dislike of American Civil War

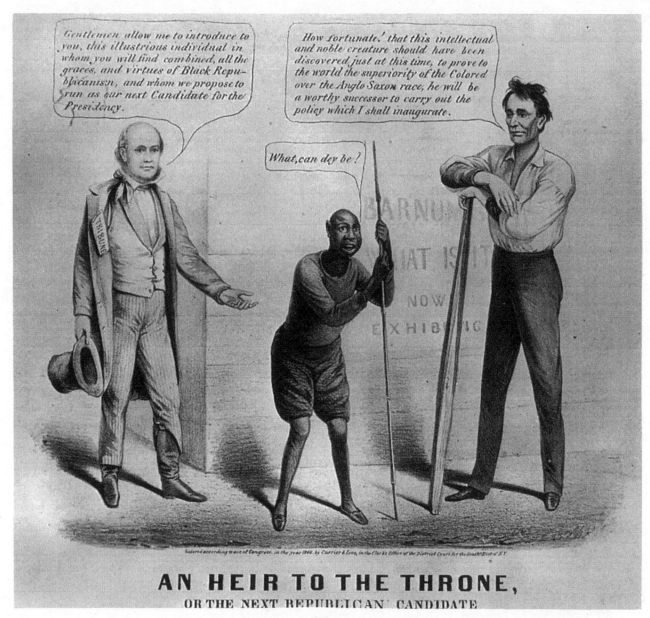

AN HEIR TO THE THRONE,
OR THE NEXT REPUBLICAN CANDIDATE

FIGURE 17. Currier & Ives, *An Heir to the Throne, Or the Next Republican Candidate*, New York (1860). Lithograph (probably by Louis Maurer), 12 × 11 ⅞ in. One of many racist anti-Lincoln cartoons, this print attacks Lincoln's chief sin in Democratic eyes, his unbending insistence that the black man was a person with certain inalienable rights, most importantly the right to the fruits of his own labor. The figure of the "What Is It?" a misshapen African, was copied from an advertisement for P. T. Barnum's "Museum," a copy of which appeared in *Frank Leslie's Illustrated Newspaper*, December 15, 1860. (*Louis A. Warren Lincoln Library and Museum*)

THE RAIL CANDIDATE.

FIGURE 18. Currier & Ives, *The Rail Candidate*, New York (1860). Lithograph (probably by Louis Maurer), 16 ½ × 11 ¾ in. Lincoln sits uncomfortably atop the Republican platform, now represented by a single rail, and admits: "It is true I have Split Rails, but I begin to feel as if *this* Rail would split me, it's the hardest stick I ever straddled." Puns, such as "straddling" the party platform, were a staple of Civil War era cartoons.
(Harry T. Peters Collection, Museum of the City of New York)

cartoons: Lincoln gets handled pretty roughly, and his subsequent canonization has made the national mind, even its aesthetic sensibilities, recoil from attacks on him.

Lincoln was not handled any more roughly than other politicians of the era, including presidents. Modern Americans simply like him more. Thus it seems silly to argue that *Vanity Fair* failed in part because of its anti-Negro cartoons. It is true that the black man's image improved briefly late in the Civil War and until the twilight of Reconstruction (when his image plummeted precipitously, especially at Currier & Ives, which then published a series of racist "Darktown" cartoons). Improvement came only after 1863, when blacks became soldiers in the Union armies, and *Vanity Fair*'s demise the same year could hardly have resulted from that. The most recent writers on American political cartoons—Stephen Hess and Milton Kaplan, Allan Nevins and Frank Weitenkampf—make comments which reveal their feeling that criticizing Lincoln was a mistake somehow symptomatic of the failing of American Civil War caricature.[41]

One thing is certain: The existence of campaign prints for

FIGURE 19. Currier & Ives, *Honest Abe Taking Them on the Half Shell*, New York (1860). Hand-colored lithograph (probably by Louis Maurer), 18 × 13⅜ in. In 1860, Republicans classified Democrats as either "hard-shell" (strongly pro-slavery) or "soft-shell" (moderate on the question). In this clever cartoon, an informally dressed Lincoln ponders which rival to swallow first, soft-shell presidential nominee Stephen A. Douglas (left) or hard-shell opponent John C. Breckinridge (right). This interesting variation on the Cooper Institute photograph (Fig. 6) finds Lincoln grinning rather uncharacteristically; he never smiled in his photographs and no one knows what his teeth looked like. Political cartoons served a more ephemeral and less decorative purpose than most Currier & Ives prints and were rarely colored. *(Louis A. Warren Lincoln and Museum)*

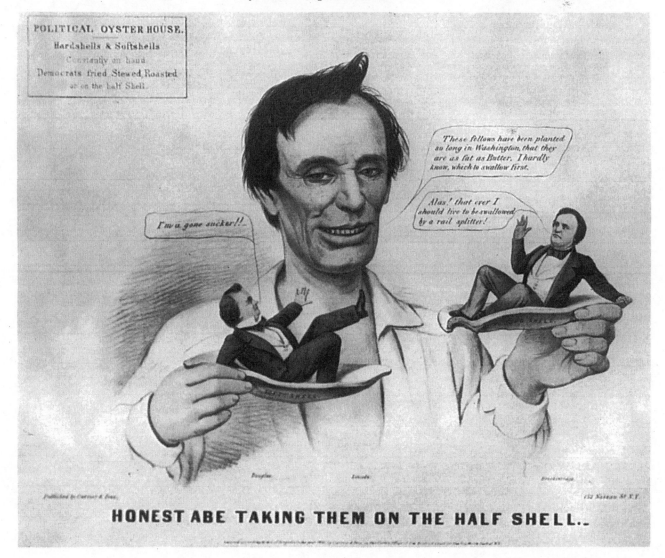

HONEST ABE TAKING THEM ON THE HALF SHELL..

FIGURE 20. [Printmaker unknown], *The Political Quadrille/Music by Dred Scott*, probably New York (1860). Lithograph 13 ¾ × 17 ⅞ in. Unusual in that it lampoons all the political parties in 1860, this fine cartoon, uncluttered by puns or language balloons, portrays (clockwise from upper right): Lincoln dancing with a black wench; John Bell (leader of the remnants of the nativist Know Nothings) dancing with a real "native" American; Stephen A. Douglas (the champion of "popular sovereignty") dancing with a "squatter sovereign;" and John C. Breckinridge dancing with the unpopular incumbent President, "Old Buck" (James Buchanan). *(Library of Congress)*

FIGURE 21. Photograph of the artist Thomas Hicks as he looked around the time he painted his Abraham Lincoln. *(Illinois State Historical Library)*

candidates regardless of party, and the existence of cartoons lampooning different sides in a party contest (sometimes drawn by the same artist) in the lists of the same publishing house prove that commercialism, not political belief, was the prime force motivating the engravers and lithographers in their rush to produce Lincoln images in 1860.

Not all the printmakers rushed. To the credit of several publishers of the period, there was an effort, beginning the month after Lincoln's nomination, to produce campaign prints of higher quality and greater originality than those based exclusively and slavishly on existing photographs. Several printmakers commissioned artists to travel to Springfield to make life portraits of the nominee upon which prints could be based. This required a far greater capital investment than the mere adaptation of photographs. Unfortunately, it also usually involved the youngest and least experienced artists of the period—those most likely to agree to pack bag, baggage, and easels for the unpleasant summertime journey to and from Lincoln's hometown by train.

One of the very first artists to come West to paint Lincoln in oils as the model for a print was Thomas Hicks (1823–1890) of

New York (Fig. 21). Seven years earlier, believing he had died in a train accident, a newspaper wrote: "The world of art has been deprived of one of its most talented members. . . ." Reports of Hicks's death had been exaggerated. He survived the wreck, and as he later recalled, "In 1860 after the nomination of Mr. Lincoln at Chicago, Mr. Schaus, the art publisher of New York, sent me to Springfield, Illinois, to paint a portrait of Mr. Lincoln to be published for the campaign of that year."[42]

Armed with a letter of introduction from the New York *Tribune*'s editorial writer Charles A. Dana to Lincoln's law partner, Hicks arrived in Springfield and proceeded to the State House, where the candidate had set up temporary offices. "Here," one of Lincoln's earliest biographers, J. G. Holland, wrote, "he met the millionaire and the menial, the priest and the politician, men, women and children. . . . From morning until night this was his business."[43] His business soon included sitting for painters, too, but he accepted the additional duty. Hicks began work on June 12, 1860.

In charming reminiscences published many years later, Hicks recalled his subject as "a tall, gaunt man, with a pleasant expression on his well-marked features." Hicks was gratified to learn that Lincoln seemed to understand the requirements of his project and endorsed it: "When he had read Dana's letter, which explained the object of my visit, he said: 'Yes, I will do in this matter what my friends in New York wish of me; and I am much obliged to you, sir, for coming so far to paint my likeness for them.' " Lincoln took "an interest in the work," Hicks recalled, and inspecting the preliminary charcoal sketch, exclaimed: "I see the likeness, sir."

FIGURE 22. Portrait from life by Thomas Hicks, signed and dated: *Painted from Life/by Thomas Hicks. Springfield Illinois/June 14h. 1860.* Oil on canvas, 20 ½ × 24 ½ in. The first life painting of Lincoln, it was commissioned by a New York print publisher specifically to serve as a model for a campaign lithograph. Lincoln's friend Orville H. Browning called it "an exact, life like likeness, and a beautiful work of art," adding, "It is deeply imbued with the intellectual and spiritual, and I doubt whether any one ever succeeds in getting a better picture of the man." (*Diary of Orville Hickman Browning*, I, 415.) (*Chicago Historical Society*)

A visitor to the State House during subsequent sittings remarked: "I suppose Mr. Lincoln, you have to give a good deal of time to this kind of work." Mr. Lincoln said: "No, this is the first time that I have had this specific sort of picture made, but I have had the sun pictures made several times." On the office wall was hanging a very dark photograph with a light background, and his guest from the East said: "I see a photograph of you there," pointing to the one on the wall, "but it does not appear to have any sun in it." "No," said Mr. Lincoln, with his peculiar smile, "Parson Brownlow says I am a nigger; and if he had judged alone from that picture, he would have had some ground for his assertion."

As work on the canvas proceeded, Lincoln became "more and more interested in its progress." Once he remarked: "It interests me to see how, by adding a touch here and a touch there, you make it look more like me. I do not understand it, but I see it is a vocation in which the work is very fine." Replied Hicks rather condescendingly: "That is the reason why painting is called one of the fine arts."[44]

In fact, Hicks's portrait was not solely the product of skill and inspiration—not truthfully an example of "the fine arts." It depended in large part on a photographic model (Fig. 23), even though his publisher's desire for a new model not made from the camera had been the reason Hicks was sent West to paint Lincoln.

Nine days before Hicks began work, the Republican National Committee, worried that reproductions of Hesler's "tousle-haired" photograph were making "Lincoln's unkempt appearance" contrast "too unfavorably with that of Douglas," had rehired the photographer to make a new, more flattering set of campaign pictures. "I went to Springfield," recalled Alexander

FIGURE 23. Photograph by Alexander Hesler, Springfield, Illinois (June 3, 1860). *(Library of Congress)*

Yours truly
A Lincoln

Hesler in his old age, "and made the negative that was afterward used for the campaign badges." But even before the photographs could be made into ferrotype badges or woven silk ribbons, Thomas Hicks selected one and, in large part, modeled his "life" portrait on this camera study, although the "original" had consented to pose from life.[45]

Lincoln supposedly liked the finished picture (Fig. 22). Mrs. Lincoln was reported to have commented: "Yes, that is Mr. Lincoln. It is exactly like him, and his friends in New York will see him as he looks at home." Lincoln's friend, Orville H. Browning wrote out an endorsement for the portrait, pronouncing it "a great success. . . . I doubt whether art is capable of transferring to canvass a more exact, and life like representation of the 'human face divine.'"[46]

Before Hicks took his final leave of Springfield, he asked the candidate to write out a brief memorandum of directions to his Kentucky birthplace. Hicks had proposed to travel there from Springfield to paint the famous log cabin, arguing, "You are to be the next President of the United States, and the people will want a picture of your birthplace." A look of "inexpressible sadness" came over Lincoln's face when he heard the request. But he regained his composure and wrote this, one of the very rare autobiographical statements from this reticent man: "I was born February 12, 1809 in then Hardin county Kentucky, at a point within the now recently formed county of Larue, a mile, or a mile & a half from where Hodgin'sville now is. My parents being dead and my own memory not serving, I know no means of identifying the precise locality. It was on Nolin Creek."[47] But for some reason Hicks did not undertake the journey to Kentucky. Instead, he packed his completed life portrait and brought it back to New

FIGURE 24. Leopold Grozelier after a life portrait by Thomas Hicks, *Hon. Abraham Lincoln* [with facsimile signature: *Yours truly/A. Lincoln*], published by W. Schaus, New York (1860). Lithograph, 20 ⅜ × 26 in. This is the Hicks portrait that curious Easterners eventually saw. Later, at least one photographer brought the project full cycle by photographing this lithograph, itself based on a photograph (Fig. 23), and issuing it as an authentic camera study of the candidate. (*Louis A. Warren Lincoln Library and Museum*)

York. There it was lithographed by Leopold Grozelier for W. Schaus (Fig. 24).

The print won considerable praise from the newspapers. The New York *Tribune* observed: "Busts, photographs, and engravings have multiplied and have deepened the impression that Mr. Lincoln was—well, not handsome. Mr. Hicks has put another face upon the question." From another newspaper critic came this comment:

> We have at last a respectful likeness of Lincoln. It is a splendid lithograph from the painting by Hicks . . . a good picture. There seems to have been a vigorous rivalry among portraitists and cartoonists in making Lincoln appear the ugliest of living men. Some of them show a coarse wrinkled personage, who does not look as if a gleam of good nature or common sense ever disturbed him. In Hicks' portrait, we have a more pleasing as well as a more accurate painting.

FIGURE 25. Portrait from life by Charles Alfred Barry, Springfield, Illinois (June 1860). Charcoal on paper, 21 × 29 in. Prominent Massachusetts Republicans commissioned Barry to create an original life portrait from which campaign prints could be made. This original was displayed in Chicago, New York, and Boston, then vanished for more than a century; it was rediscovered recently. This is its first publication in a book. (*Memorial Hall Library, Andover, Massachusetts*)

According to Hicks, Lincoln himself said of the effort, "I think the picture has a somewhat pleasanter expression than I usually have, but that, perhaps is not an objection." He had accurately predicted the reaction with which his "New York friends" would greet the appearance of the lithograph.[48]

Hicks had accomplished his purpose. Other painters would fare less well in modeling life portraits from which prints could be made for the Eastern audiences. Just before Hicks began working, Charles Alfred Barry (1830–1892), a Massachusetts public school drawing master, arrived in Springfield on commission from a Boston lithographer. Young Barry presented Lincoln with a letter of introduction from Governor Nathaniel Banks, and the candi-

date, ever willing to pose but evidently growing busier in his State House labors, responded impatiently. Barry described the scene: " 'They want my head, do they?' he [Lincoln] asked, twisting my letter of introduction in his hands. 'Well, if you can get it you may have it, that is, if you are able to take it off while I am on the jump; but don't fasten me into a chair.' "

Lincoln offered to sit "at seven o'clock sharp" in his office, half expecting that no Boston artist could rouse himself at "cock-crowing." But Barry surprised him by arriving on time, produced his crayon portrait (Fig. 25) by the morning sunlight, and later recalled:

> How vividly it all comes back to me—the lonely room, the great bony figure with its long arms and legs that seemed to be continually twisting themselves together; the long, wiry neck; the narrow chest, the uncombed hair; the cavernous sockets beneath the high forehead; the bushy eyebrows hanging like curtains over the bright, dreamy eyes, the awkward speech, the evident sincerity and patience . . . that wonderful face which in its entire construction was extraordinary.
>
> But the eyes I looked upon so often never can be fully described by human language. They were not remarkable for constant brightness—on the contrary were dreamy and melancholy, always so when at rest, but could become, in an instant, when moved by some great thought, like coals of living fire. I have seen the eyes of Webster and Choate, of Macready, Forrest and the elder Booth, when they startled and awed the beholder, but I have never seen in all the wanderings of a varied life, such eyes as Lincoln had.[49]

Barry noticed something else as well: "His head was Jacksonian in shape, and the angle of the jaw all that nature intended that it should be as a sign of power and determination." In fact, the finished crayon bears a striking resemblance to several period paintings of Old Hickory, a similarity at least one critic would later observe.

Like so many artists who wrote reminiscences, Barry insisted that Lincoln thought his portrait "a true likeness." To modern eyes, however, there is more Jackson than Lincoln in it. Perhaps any Massachusetts artist was likely to be looking for a Jackson in any Western presidential candidate. But there was more to it than that. To some, the times seemed to demand a Jackson to face down Southern secession threats. When later those threats became real and Lincoln, as President-elect, remained still unproven, the reporter Henry Villard predicted hopefully, " . . . there are dormant qualities in 'Old Abe' which occasion will draw forth, develop and remind people to a certain degree of the characteristics of 'Old Hickory.' " A Boston newspaper critic commented when Barry's picture was briefly displayed there: "There is apparently enough of the General Jackson firmness to please the most ardent admirer of 'Old Hickory,' and withal a pleasant, genial expression of the 'How d'ye do? Make yourself at home' order, that evinces a readiness of adaptation to any circumstance, even though that circumstance be the Presidential Chair . . . it is to be engraved at once in the best possible manner, and will have a large sale."[50]

The critic's prediction proved wrong on three counts. The crayon was not engraved, but lithographed (Fig. 26). The manner in which it was adapted was adequate but not "the best." And its rarity today suggests it was anything but a best seller in 1860. The print was made quickly, and by July 22 a rival artist had already

FIGURE 26. J[oseph]. E. Baker after a life portrait by Charles Alfred Barry, *Abraham Lincoln* (with facsimile signature: *Yours truly/A. Lincoln*), published by J[ohn] H. Bufford's Lith., Boston (1860). Lithograph, 20 ¼ × 27 ⅝ in. A Boston newspaper predicted that this stylized print would "have a large sale." And artist Barry thought Baker's lithographic adaptation "better then anything Grozelier (see Fig. 24] *ever* did" (Barry to George W. Nichols [1860]. Louis A. Warren Lincoln Library and Museum). Very few of the prints were published, however, possibly because the lithographic stone broke early on in the printing process. (R. Gerald McMurtry, *Beardless Portraits of Abraham Lincoln Painted from Life*, pp. 10, 12–13.) Interestingly, the image may have achieved its widest circulation in a number of pirated editions issued by rival printmakers, both in separate sheets and for at least one picture newspaper. *(Louis A. Warren Lincoln Library and Museum)*

seen the lithograph and declared it a "failure." Perhaps the haste with which it was published accounted for its lack of success. Writing from Springfield, the rival declared: "Everybody laughs at B's lith. In this city—it is very unpopular." To his mind, "Barry's original drawing is like him in very many respects but the lithograph from it is a failure."[51]

The print should logically have been the best of the entire campaign. The lithographer was Joseph E. Baker, who had worked for the publisher for ten years and was "a very competent artist,"[52] in the words of lithograph expert Harry Twyford Peters. The publisher was John H. Bufford, about whom a Boston newspaper would later write: "Bufford's lithographs are sold wherever the flag of our country waves. . . and have carried into the homes of the people the rarest gems of modern art. . . ." It was Bufford, the notice declared, who had proven "invaluable in educating the people up to a true taste, and in fostering their love for the beautiful."[53] But not this time.

Somehow none of the principals involved in the Lincoln effort had managed to save the project from misfiring. It got off to a rousing start when the sketch was displayed on an easel surrounded by flags and flowers at a Massachusetts Republican rally and provoked, Barry claimed, "the wildest enthusiasm." Other clubs wanted the picture, too. Barry knew that there was "unquestionably a *heap* of money behind the head for all concerned." In the end, however, the lithograph was priced at three dollars, and only "families of means" could afford one. Perhaps Barry himself came closest to explaining the failure when he admitted in his memoir that he had experienced "no end of trouble in getting the expression I wanted of his mouth—of the whole lower part of his

face, in fact—his countenance changed so quickly.''[54] Unlike Hicks, Barry had not consulted a photograph.

The artist who had written so disparagingly of the Barry-Baker-Bufford collaboration fared no better in his own subsequent effort to create an original life model for a print. Nonetheless, his experiences provide one of the most fascinating case studies of all the print productions of the Lincoln era.

Thomas M. Johnston (1834–1869) was the son of David Claypoole Johnston, the "American Cruikshank," whose reputation as a caricaturist was known across the nation. In July 1860, the publisher C. H. Brainard hired young Johnston to make the trip to Springfield to paint Lincoln from the flesh. How much period printmakers staked upon the efficient and inspired creation of these likenesses is reflected in surviving correspondence between the artist and his patron.

Welcoming Johnston, Lincoln "consented to sit . . . without the least hesitation," the painter reported in a letter, adding in a later note: "I feel sure of getting a good thing." First of all, Johnston needed cash—he found himself with only "27 dollars in pocket."[55] His publisher was long on sympathy but apparently short on funds: "The picture buyers must be dead or out of town," he complained. In order to advance money to his artist, Brainard had to leave "1,000 small portraits of Douglas" with a Chicago company as collateral. "Greater than Moses, who brought water from a rock," he reported, "I extract money from Lithographic Stones, and enclose *Ten dollars.*"

Along with the money came Brainard's advice that the Lincoln painting should "not only be a characteristic likeness but a pleasing picture. All the pictures that have yet been issued leave an unfavorable impression upon the minds of the spectators. I feel

quite confident that your picture will be *the* picture of *the* man."
"Don't forget," he lectured, "to get all the testimonials you can as
to the accuracy, etc. of your portrait. 'We must keep blowing' and
thus make the public shell out. I feel certain that everybody will
be *clamorous* for the picture, as it is *meet* they should be, considering how much we have *staked* upon it."[56]

Despite the cash and the letters of encouragement, Johnston
did little more than copy a photograph (Figs. 27, 28). Perhaps he
set too high a goal—making "a likeness that every Republican will
have reason to be proud of." Perhaps he simply did not possess
the talent to convey his view that Lincoln's face was "beautiful in
the extreme, when compared with all the pictures that have been
published over his name." "The picture is a decided success,"
Johnston wrote to his father as he prepared to return home. One
can only speculate about how the elder Johnston and the ambitious print publisher reacted when they finally saw the canvas.
Though undisguisedly modeled after a two-year-old photograph,
it was idealized: Johnston had made Lincoln's ears smaller, abbre-
viated his mouth, and added a darker color to his translucent,
light gray eyes. Even Lincoln's jutting cheekbone was whittled
away. When Brainard lithographed it, however, he may have
worked from the photograph and not the canvas: many of the
subtle alterations imposed by Johnston were corrected. For years,
only the print portrait (Fig. 29) was known to us. The painting
vanished in 1860 and Johnston died young, leaving the location
of the picture a family secret. It was not until 1983 that it was
rediscovered. It is published in this book for the first time anywhere, the latest of several long-lost 1860 Lincoln campaign
portraits to resurface this century.[57]

A print designed to appeal to the voters of Pennsylvania fared

far better. State Supreme Court Judge John Meredith Read of
Philadelphia, a strong Lincoln supporter, hired the renowned
miniaturist John Henry Brown (1818–1891) to travel to Springfield and portray the candidate in a more romanticized vein than
had been evident in most engravings and lithographs. Brown was
one of the last practitioners of a vanishing art.[58] As a colleague of
his later explained to William H. Seward: "My business as a
miniature painter, which in former days throve, has from month
to month been dying, on account of the increasing popularity of
photographing, which you will no doubt know monopolizes the
legitimate business of artists."[59]

Lincoln's private secretary, John G. Nicolay, understood precisely the nature of Brown's mission to Springfield. In a letter to
his fiancée, he wrote:

FIGURE 28. Portrait from life by
Thomas M. Johnston, Springfield,
Illinois, signed and dated: "T.M.J.
1860." Oil on canvas 22 ⅝ × 17 ⅜
in oval. Although the artist enjoyed
life sittings, he all but copied an old
photograph (Fig. 27). *(Hirschl & Adler
Galleries/Helga Photo Studio)*

A. Lincoln.

ABRAHAM LINCOLN.

Published by C.H. BRAINARD Boston 1860.

Judge Read of Philadelphia ... has become so disgusted with the horrible caricatures of Mr. Lincoln which he had seen that he went to the expense of sending this artist all the way out here to paint this picture, and which will probably cost him some $300, the price of the painting alone being $175. I had a long talk with the artist today. He says that the impression prevails East that Mr. Lincoln is very ugly an impression which the published pictures of him of course all confirm. Read however had an idea that it could hardly be so—but was bound to have a good looking picture, and therefore instructed the artist to make it good looking whether the original would justify it or not.

Nicolay was delighted with the result (Fig. 31), based wholly on a specially commissioned ambrotype (Fig. 30) made for the artist's use in Springfield. He added to his fiancée: "Did you ever see a real, pretty miniature? I do not mean either an ambrotype, a daguerreotype or photograph, but a regular *miniature painted* on ivory. Well, a Philadelphia artist (Brown, his name is), has just been painting one of Mr. Lincoln, which is both very pretty and very truthful—decidedly the best picture of him that I have seen."[60]

Mrs. Lincoln also admired the portrait, writing a strong letter of endorsement describing the miniature likeness as "perfect" and adding, "I see no fault or defect whatever." Lincoln himself wrote to Judge Read (see Fig. 33) that the portrait seemed "an excellent one, so far as I can judge. To my unpracticed eye, it is without fault." Brown, too, seemed pleased. He noted in his diary that the "people of Springfield ... speak of it in strong terms of approbation, declaring it to be the best that has yet been taken of him."[61]

FIGURE 29. C. H. Brainard after a portrait from life by Thomas M. Johnston, *Abraham Lincoln* [with facsimile signature: *A. Lincoln*], Boston (1860). The lithograph seemed to be based more on the German photograph (Fig. 27) than the Johnston painting (Fig. 28). The publisher, who had to surrender a batch of prints of Douglas as collateral to keep his business afloat and pay Johnston's expenses in Springfield, might just as well have purchased a copy of the German photo himself for a few pennies. Lithograph, 10 ¾ × 13 ⅞ in. (*Louis A. Warren Lincoln Library and Museum*)

THE GENESIS OF ONE PRINT PORTRAIT OF LINCOLN

THE PHOTOGRAPH BECOMES A PAINTING

FIGURE 30. An ambrotype by Preston Butler, Springfield, Illinois (August 13, 1860), one of a series taken for the artist John Henry Brown to use in making a life portrait commissioned as a model for a campaign engraving. *(Lloyd Ostendorf Collection)*

FIGURE 31. Miniature from life by John Henry Brown, Springfield, Illinois (August 16–25, 1860). Watercolor on ivory, 4 ½ × 5 ½ in. The miniature became the property of Judge John M. Read, who had commissioned it. He later gave it to Mary Todd Lincoln, and it remained in the Lincoln family for more than a century. It is now in the National Portrait Gallery. *(National Portrait Gallery, Smithsonian Institution)*

ENGRAVED BY SAMUEL SARTAIN AFTER THE MINIATURE BY M. W. HALL, CHICAGO, 1860

A. Lincoln

AND THE PAINTING BASED ON THE PHOTOGRAPH
BECOMES A PRINT FOR THE PEOPLE

FIGURE 32. Samuel Sartain after a life portrait by John Henry Brown, *A. Lincoln* [facsimile signature], published by James Irwin, Philadelphia (1860). Mezzotint engraving, 4 × 5 3/8 in. Sartain's straightforward adaptation of "the miniature from life by J. Henry Brown in the possession of Judge Read" bore one of the most precise caption acknowledgments in the body of Lincoln print portraiture. The costly effort had progressed from a photograph by Butler to miniature by Brown to engraving by Sartain. The process took three months. *(Mr. and Mrs. G.S. Boritt)*

FIGURE 33. Lincoln endorsement of the John Henry Brown portrait from life. *(Library of Congress)*

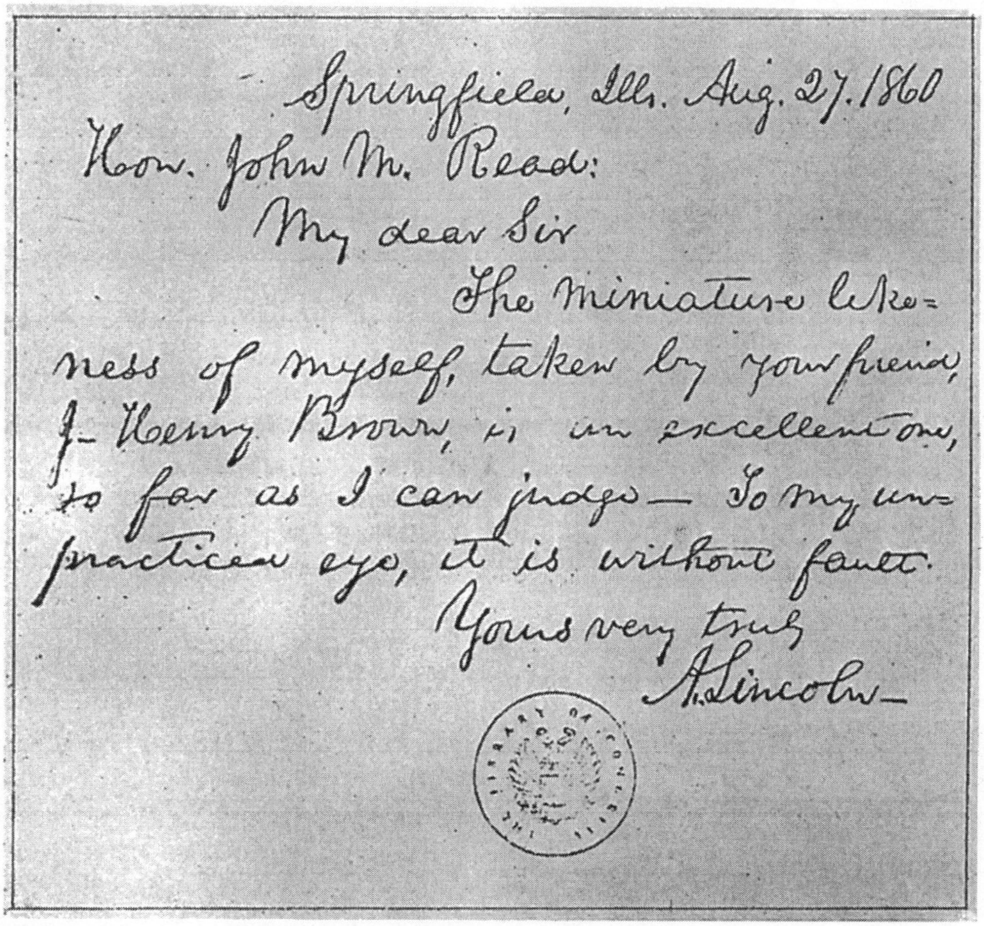

Springfield, Ills. Aug. 27. 1860
Hon. John M. Read:
My dear Sir
The miniature likeness of myself, taken by your friend, J. Henry Brown, is an excellent one, so far as I can judge— To my unpracticed eye, it is without fault.
Yours very truly
A. Lincoln—

It was no wonder, then, that Nicolay was eager for the miniature to be engraved and circulated in Pennsylvania, a key swing state scheduled to hold its state elections a month before the presidential vote. By late September the print had still not been published. Finally, John Henry Brown wrote to Nicolay about "the steel engraving from my picture of Mr. Lincoln."

> Mr. Sartain [Samuel Sartain, a noted Philadelphia engraver] promised to have it completed in two weeks after the picture was placed in his hands, which was on last Monday three weeks ago.

Two days ago the first proof was placed in my hands for criticism. . . . Today I will again examine it with care, and if necessary will have such further corrections made as my judgement may suggest. In accordance with my promise to you I will not allow any copies to be issued until they meet my approbation.

Judge Read is in a nervous condition at Sartain's delay. He thinks the engraving good, & wanted some copies yesterday, but as I am *judge* in this case, I would not consent.

As soon as the plate is ready for printing from, which I think will be tomorrow or on Monday next, copies will be sent to you without delay.[62]

In fact, it was not until mid-October that copies of the print (Fig. 32) finally arrived in Springfield for Lincoln's inspection. He acknowledged the "two framed engravings" in a note in Nicolay's handwriting. By this time, as Lincoln remarked, "the late splendid victories in Pennsylvania" and other states seemed "to foreshadow the certain success of the Republican cause in November."[63] Here was one print portrait that may have been issued too late to make much difference.

Whatever its impact on Lincoln's ultimate victory in Pennsylvania, the Brown-Sartain collaboration proved typical of the politically commissioned likenesses of the period, portraits for expedience and not for posterity. The print no more accurately reflected the way Lincoln really looked during that summer in Springfield than his bland and noncontroversial statements of those weeks reflected his true attitude toward policy issues. Brown's was a glimpse of the man his wife and friends—and perhaps even Lincoln himself—wished him to be, not necessarily the man as he really was.

There is no way accurately to know how many printed images

of Abraham Lincoln were reproduced in quantity and circulated through the North during the campaign of 1860, original images as well as piracies and fakes (see Figs. 34, 35). Such records were seldom kept even by the most businesslike of the publishers. The surviving evidence constitutes a rich archive that embraces alike the crude and careful likenesses; the simplistic, disguised, or idealized adaptations of photographs; the naive music sheets and the gaudy posters; and the prints for which life paintings were commissioned. All of these suggest a healthy trade in Lincoln prints during that first presidential campaign. A disgruntled agent for Barry's expensive portrait commented on the eve of the election that "the country is *flooded* with the pictures of Lincoln, in all conceivable shapes and sizes, and *cheap*. The newspapers have his likeness; it is in the medal form; it is on envelopes; it is on badges; it is on cards; it is, indeed, on every thing, and every where. And all for a *few cents!* . . . The most miserable likeness of Lincoln, with a plenty of *color*, if cheap, will go like buckwheat cakes."

What is difficult to calculate is the extent to which Lincoln or his advisers depended on the distribution of these portraits or understood their power. They knew enough to shower the Wigwam with hastily printed woodcuts. But did they know more? They seem to have been catching on. When Norman B. Judd, one of Lincoln's political lieutenants in Illinois, wrote the nominee in June to request a profile photograph for a medal maker in Philadelphia, he said: "Every little [bit] helps, and I am coming to believe that likenesses broad cast, are excellent means of electioneering."[64]

Under ordinary circumstances, Lincoln's election should have put a halt to the mass production of new printed portraits. But

A PREWAR PRINT WITH JOHN C. CALHOUN . . .

FIGURE 34. Henry S. Sadd after a painting by Tompkins Harrison Matteson (1813–1884), *Union*, published by William Pate, New York (1852). Mezzotint engraving, 29 ⅜ × 22 ¼ in. This print celebrated the political consensus arrived at by the Compromise of 1850, uniting "The Great Compromiser" Henry Clay with New England's Daniel Webster and South Carolina's John C. Calhoun, as well as other prominent politicians. *(Louis A. Warren Lincoln Library and Museum)*

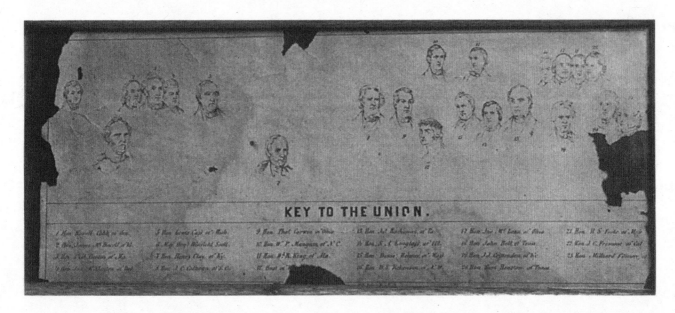

... BECOMES A PRINT WITH ABRAHAM LINCOLN

FIGURE 35. [Printmaker unknown], *Union*, second state of the original engraving by Henry Sadd after a painting by Matteson. Probably New York (*c.* 1861). Steel plates endure, but politics change rapidly. To renew the marketability of this print nearly a decade after its original printing, several of the faces of the principal figures in the original had to be burnished out and replaced by portraits of more pro-Union public figures. The principal revision finds the head of Calhoun supplanted by a crudely drawn Lincoln (center), the portrait based on the Brady "Cooper Institute" photograph (Fig. 6). In addition, Edward Everett (far left) replaces Howell Cobb; W. P. Magnum and William R. King (both seen beneath the outstretched left arm of the angel at top) are replaced by William H. Seward and Benjamin F. Butler; and Major Robert Anderson (directly above the right ear on the Washington bust) is substituted for James Buchanan. The inclusion of Anderson, "hero" of the fall of Fort Sumter in April 1861, suggests that this print was not issued until sometime thereafter, even though Lincoln is portrayed here as clean-shaven. A third edition of the engraving, this time with Lincoln bearded, was published subsequently but possibly not until after his assassination in 1865. (*Library of Congress*)

when Lincoln began growing whiskers soon thereafter, he rendered all the beardless engravings and lithographs of himself obsolete. Had he not grown his beard, publishers would have been able to reissue their campaign prints with revised captions reflecting Lincoln's newly earned status as President-elect. Now, further alterations would be required, and quickly.

No one knows for sure why Lincoln decided, as he approached his fifty-second birthday, to grow a beard for the first time in his life. There is at least some evidence to suggest that he did so in response to rather direct suggestions that whiskers would improve his appearance. From one such correspondent came this advice in October of 1860:

> To the
> Hon. Abm. Lincoln
>   Dear Sir
>   Allow a number of very earnest Republicans to intimate to you, that after oft-repeated views of the daguerreotypes; which we wear as tokens of our devotedness to you; we have come to the candid determination that these medals would be much improved in appearance, provided you would cultivate whiskers and wear standing collars.
>   Believe us nothing but an earnest desire that "our candidate" should be the best looking as well as the best of the rival candidates, would induce us to trespass upon your valued time.
> your Most
sincere & earnest
well wishers
True Republicans
>
> P.S. We really fear votes will be lost to "the cause" unless our "gentle hints" are attended to.[65]

There is no record of Lincoln's reaction to that letter, but there is Lincoln's now legendary response to the letter from an eleven-year-old admirer from upstate New York. It was written on October 15.

> NY
> Westfield Chatauque Co
> Oct 15, 1860
>
> Hon A B Lincoln
> Dear Sir
> My father has just home from the fair and brought home your picture and Mr. Hamlin's. I am a little girl only eleven years old, but want you should be President of the United States very much so I hope you wont think me very bold to write to such a great man as you are. . . . I have got 4 brother's and part of them will vote for you any way and if you will let your whiskers grow I will try and get the rest of them to vote for you you would look a great deal better for your face is so thin. All the ladies like whiskers and they would tease their husband's to vote for you and then you would be President. . . . I think that rail fence around your picture makes it look very pretty. . . .
>
> Grace Bedell

Four days later, Lincoln responded:

> Springfield, Ills.
> Oct 19. 1860
>
> Miss. Grace Bedell
> My dear little Miss.
> Your very agreeable letter of the 15th. is received. . . .
> As to the whiskers, having never worn any, do you not think people would call it a piece of silly affect[at]ion if I were to begin it now? Your very sincere well-wisher
> A. Lincoln.[66]

NATIONAL REPUBLICAN CHART

PRESIDENTIAL CAMPAIGN, 1860

The technique here was one that President Lincoln, as a skilled politician, was to use in the future. He would acknowledge the criticism, offer an objection to it which seemed proof that he did not accept it, and then do precisely what the critic asked.

Because of Grace Bedell's description of a rail fence border on the Lincoln-Hamlin image that inspired her, it has generally been believed that a Lincoln print portrait, specifically the centerpiece of H. H. Lloyd's *National Republican Chart* (Fig. 36), in effect, caused the printmakers so many later problems. There is some poetic justice in the fact that Lincoln's tonsorial decision may have been "inspired" by a print likeness. Grace Bedell's precise influence on Lincoln is unclear; but the poster's influence on *her* is indisputable, and indicative of the importance such images held for the picture-hungry society of the 1860s.

This was the first time a presidential candidate had altered his appearance between his election and his inauguration, and public curiosity was ablaze. Unfortunately, the printmakers were so unprepared that, from all evidence, none sent artists to Springfield to record the change in Lincoln's appearance. Besides, the election was already over. So, for the most part, they guessed haphazardly at the style of beard Lincoln ultimately might affect, and published these pictorial forecasts in a variety of sizes, shapes, textures, and shades, usually engraving or lithographing a beard onto an existing plate or stone without comparing the resulting image to new photographs of Lincoln. Most printmakers had evidently determined that nothing could be worse than not adding beards to their new Lincoln portraits, no matter how uncharacteristic the beards they added. Only a few firms issued portraits whose captions identified Lincoln as President but which depicted him as clean-shaven.[67]

FIGURE 36. H. H. Lloyd, *National Republican Chart/Presidential Campaign, 1860*, New York (1860). Colored, wood-engraved broadside with type, 25 ¾ × 34 in. A comprehensive partisan guide to the 1860 campaign, this broadside features, among other details, quotes from Lincoln speeches, biographies of the presidential and vice-presidential candidates, the full text of the party platform, and portraits not only of Lincoln (based on Brady, Fig. 6) and Hamlin, but of all fifteen previous presidents (who look strangely alike in these roughly engraved sketches). Printmaker Lloyd also issued a *Democratic Chart* as well as a nonpartisan version featuring all the presidential candidates, testimony to the nonaffiliated commercialism of most print publishers of the period. After the war the design was used for the *National Political Chart*, featuring portraits of Lincoln along with his military and cabinet officers. (*Louis A. Warren Lincoln Library and Museum*)

ABRAHAM LINCOLN.

FIGURE 37. L[ouis]. Prang after a drawing by A. K. Kipps, *Abraham Lincoln,* Boston, (*c.* 1861). Lithograph, 6 × 7 ⅞ in. Forced to respond quickly to public demand for portraits of the newly bearded President-elect, printmakers produced wildly varying interpretations, mostly guesswork, in the absence of photographic models. One of the most amusing, this Prang lithograph, based on the timeworn 1857 Hesler photograph (Fig. 2), features a Lincoln with mutton-chop sidewhiskers but no beard. A second state of the print offered Lincoln in full whiskers—too full, in fact. (*Harold Holzer*)

One print (Fig. 37) by Louis Prang (1824–1909, see Fig. 38) portrayed Lincoln with sidewhiskers, which was more inaccurate than Currier & Ives's attempt to update its classic campaign portrait (Fig. 39) with the superimposition of a beard (Fig. 40) far fuller than any Lincoln ever wore. Most guesses were marketable, and they were cheaper, faster, and less troublesome than a conscientious return to the drawing board.[68]

The "bearding" of the prints of Lincoln marked the print industry's first attempt to adapt to Lincoln's changing image. Soon some of the printmakers would have to abandon their "rail old Western gentleman." He was no longer the homey former backwoodsman, "Honest Old Abe," but the leader of a nation facing deep and unprecedented crisis.

No one, least among them the engravers and lithographers, could have anticipated what lay ahead as Abraham Lincoln began his long journey to Washington to take the oath of office as President. On February 16, his inaugural train reached Westfield, New York, where Lincoln greeted a crowd of well-wishers and then announced: "Some three months ago, I received a letter from a young lady here; it was a very pretty letter, and she advised

Aincoln.
HON. ABRAHAM LINCOLN.
REPUBLICAN CANDIDATE FOR
SIXTEENTH PRESIDENT OF THE UNITED STATES.

THE LINCOLN "IMAGE," BEFORE AND AFTER

FIGURE 39. Currier & Ives, *Hon. Abraham Lincoln,/Republican Candidate for/Sixteenth President of the United States* [with facsimile signature: *A. Lincoln*], New York (1860). Lithograph 14 × 18 ¾ in. First,

Currier & Ives published this straightforward interpretation of Mathew Brady's "Cooper Institute" photograph (Fig. 6). *(Louis A. Warren Lincoln Library and Museum)*

A. Lincoln
HON. ABRAHAM LINCOLN.
SIXTEENTH PRESIDENT OF THE UNITED STATES.

THE PRINT "GROWS" WHISKERS

FIGURE 40. Currier & Ives, *Hon. Abraham Lincoln./Sixteenth President of the United States* [with facsimile signature: *A. Lincoln*], New York (1861). Lithograph, 14 × 18 ¾ in. To update the print, Currier & Ives artists removed the second line of the original caption ("Republican Candidate For") and added a thick, bushy beard. One wonders how pleased photographer Mathew Brady might have been to discover that the caption crediting his "Cooper Institute" photograph as the model for the beardless lithograph was retained for this revision. In a sense, the credit no longer applied and might even have proved embarrassing. (*Louis A. Warren Lincoln Library and Museum*)

me to let my whiskers grow, as it would improve my personal appearance; acting partly upon her suggestion, I have done so; and now, if she is here, I would like to see her."

Reported a newspaper correspondent on the scene: "The President left the car, and the crowd making way for him, he reached her, and gave her several hearty kisses, and amid the yells of delight from the excited crowd, he bade her good-bye, and on we rushed."[69] Grace Bedell, the little girl who had viewed a print of Lincoln and disliked it enough to suggest that Lincoln could look better, had received her deserved reward.

So had Abraham Lincoln. Commenting on the bevy of campaign portraits to a visiting newspaperman, "He referred playfully to the various 'attempts upon his life,' and the poor success that attended some of them. His greatest grievance[s] were with the artists; he tried in vain to recognize himself in some of the 'Abraham Lincolns' of the pictorials."[70] But the pictures had done him some good. More people knew him now, and more seemed willing to forgive his looks, as a printer in Philadelphia did by putting this verse below a small engraved portrait of Lincoln on a decorative envelope:

> *What though it be a homely face?—*
> *It masks a soul that never quails—*
> *A soul in purpose pure and strong,—*
> *Defending right, denouncing wrong:*
> *God speed our brave splitter of rails.*[71]

PART II

The Art of War

But the artist keeps right on, firm of heart and hand, drawing his outlines with an unwavering pencil, beautifying and idealizing our rude, material life, and thus manifesting that we have an indefeasible claim to a more enduring national existence.

—Nathaniel Hawthorne, describing a visit with artist Emanuel Leutze in Washington during the Civil War[1]

T HE CIVIL WAR was good for the arts—or so at least people in the North thought at the time. "*Inter arma non silent artes,*" exclaimed *Harper's Weekly,* as the cornerstone for the new Academy of Design was laid in New York City in 1863. "The fine arts are still eloquent amidst the roar of cannon and through the thick smoke of battle rises slowly and steadily the rich and well-proportioned building, the new Academy of Design." The orator on the occasion noted that "the great civil strifes among nations have been the tempestuous spring and seed-time for the glorious summer of all manner of intellectual fruits." Like Nathaniel Hawthorne, *Harper's* realized that such investments in the arts showed a "care that the future of the country which they intended to redeem should abound in every influence of beauty and truth." Buying a picture of a Northern hero, like subscribing to the construction of the Academy, was a "measure of the confidence" of the buyer "in the maintenance of the Union." They were both "proofs of the national purpose and faith and spirit."[2]

The *American Annual Cyclopaedia* included an entry on the fine arts for the first time in the volume covering the events of 1865. "During the recent war," said the anonymous author,

> the Fine Arts witnessed a very considerable development in the United States, the result in part of the intellectual activity which the contest promoted, and in very considerable degree also of the abundance and wide diffusion of paper money. Contrary to general expectation, painters and sculptors found a ready market for their productions, and at one period the mania for collecting became so prevalent that large numbers of pictures by modern European artists were imported into the country, and sold at what seemed enormous prices even in the inflated currency which formed the circulating medium.

Record auction prices for continental European works were set early in 1864. American artists benefited, too, obtaining higher prices and more commissions than they could execute immediately. "Thus," continued the article, "contrary to general expectation, but not contrary to the experience of other nations under similar conditions, art flourished during a civil war of unexampled magnitude to a degree never before witnessed in the country . . ."[3]

Yet most contemporary critics lamented that the war failed to stimulate much war painting. Reviewing the annual exhibition of the National Academy in New York in the spring of 1865, the critic from *Harper's Weekly* found the "number of portraits . . . fortunately not unreasonable" and the "landscapes . . . various and interesting." "But," he added, "we should gladly have seen more works inspired by the war, which is so profuse in romance, tragedy, and comedy." *The American Annual Cyclopaedia* echoed these critical principles:

At the commencement of the war American paintings were practised almost exclusively in three departments, landscape, portraiture, and *genre*, the first named being cultivated much more extensively than the other two; and the close of the struggle found the practice relatively the same. . . . Scarcely a picture of the large, historic type familiar to European galleries has issued from the studio of an American painter; and of the few battle pieces or pictures illustrating the dramatic episodes of the war which have been painted, nearly all were the work of foreign artists residing in the country. Humorous incidents, however, and subjects suggested by the camp, the bivouac, or the march, have found some capable illustrators. The tragic or pathetic element, except as developed in the numerous clever designs for the illustrated newspapers, seems to be that with which the artistic mind of the country is unable or unwilling to grapple.[4]

The critic was correct about the role of the artist-illustrators. "There was never a war before," boasted *Harper's Weekly*, "of which the varying details, the striking and picturesque scenes, the sieges, charges, and battles by land and sea, and all the innumerable romantic incidents of a great struggle have been presented to the eye of the world by the most skillful and devoted artists."[5] In addition to the work of the illustrated papers, the war also led to promotion of the arts on a grand scale and in a way ignored by the *Cyclopaedia*'s otherwise shrewd critic. The United States Sanitary Commission, a vast private relief effort which sent supplies to the soldiers in the field and aided the wounded, was the unlikely agent in this. By late 1863 the commission hit upon the idea of "sanitary fairs," gigantic charity bazaars on the scale of a modern state fair, to raise money for its cause. Along with the captured Confederate battle flags, pickles, plows, lingerie, and livestock, art proved to be one of the major attractions.

The first of these fairs was held in Chicago. Women canvassed the city for loans of artworks from private collections, gathering more than three hundred, as well as paintings completed by artists for the fair to be sold there. In addition to old masters, Frederick Edwin Church, Jasper Cropsey, Asher B. Durand, Sanford Robinson Gifford, and John F. Kensett were represented. Above the gallery for paintings and sculpture was a hall for photographs, watercolors, and steel engravings. Twenty-five thousand people visited the art gallery. Art-hungry visitors purchased seven thousand catalogues in the first five days. To satisfy popular demand, the gallery was kept open for two weeks after the other departments of the fair had closed.[6]

Philadelphia's fair in the summer of 1864 exhibited some fifteen hundred works of art. Attendance was estimated to be twelve thousand people a day, and the chairman of the art gallery committee claimed that it was the largest gallery ever seen in America. There were similar art exhibits in the Cincinnati and New York fairs. And Brooklyn's successful fair included the usual paintings, loaned and donated, Henry Ward Beecher's collection of Italian engravings, and a trompe l'oeil painting by W. T. Davis called *The Neglected Picture*, which represented "a lithograph of Jeff. Davis in an old pine frame, and with the glass broken and shivered, leaving only jagged points, and so well done as to quite deceive many a passer by, who wonders why such a shabby old affair should have been allowed to find a place here."[7]

The book departments at the sanitary fairs sold photographs of prominent men and framed lithographs and engravings as well as books. The thirst for visual representations of the events of the war was considerable, and the arts were able to provide them for all classes, but especially, it seems, for the middle and lower. "All over the country," noted *Harper's Weekly*, "thousands and thousands of the faces and events which the war has made illustrious are tacked and pinned and pasted upon the humblest walls." Many of these survive today for a reason best explained by the promoters of the Brooklyn Sanitary Fair, who attributed the easy sale of an autograph album containing signatures and letters of President Lincoln, his cabinet, generals, statesmen, and other notables to this motive: ". . . a hundred years hence, should this volume be preserved, it will be valued at thousands of dollars, as

FIGURE 41. Kimmel & Forster, *The Outbreak of the Rebellion in the United States, 1861,* New York (1865). Lithograph, 24 ½ × 16 ⅞ in. One of a series of allegorical history prints the firm of Kimmel & Forster published after the Civil War, this lithograph reflects the Republican version of the war, with a special prominence given to the con-tributions of the capitalists who pour out their treasure at Lincoln's and Liberty's feet. Southerner John Floyd, a member of James Buchanan's cabinet accused of financial corruption, greedily rakes in the coins across the splitting countryside. Jefferson Davis and his Vice-President, Alexander H. Stephens, are portrayed just behind the tearing flag. The broken shackle anachronistically refers to the abolition of slavery. James Buchanan slumbers through the crisis. To the printmakers' credit, they based Lincoln's portrait on an 1861 photograph rather than one of the more popular ones made by Brady's studio in 1864. *(Louis A. Warren Lincoln Library and Museum)*

containing the names of the men who took an important part in the greatest revolution of modern times.''[8]

To purchase a lithograph or engraving of Lincoln was still primarily a partisan action, but one that, after the firing on Fort Sumter, carried with it the special weight of a vote of confidence in the outcome of the greatest war in American history (see Fig. 41). When Lincoln announced the preliminary Emancipation Proclamation on September 22, 1862, he ensured that the war would indeed be the greatest revolution in America since 1776.

Lincoln announced it exactly one month after he had seemed to tell Horace Greeley (and through Greeley, the American people) that he would do no such thing. Ralph Waldo Emerson, an optimist turned deeply pessimistic before the issuance of the proclamation ("Life in America had lost much of its attraction in the later years."), accurately registered the "extreme moderation with which the President advanced to his design . . . so reticent that his decision has taken all parties by surprise."[9] Lincoln astonished nearly everybody, from the members of his own cabinet to printmakers.

In the case of the Emancipation Proclamation, familiarity has bred historical contempt, and it requires another considerable leap of historical imagination to recapture the real grandeur of that document. Richard Hofstadter, in one of the most influential pieces on Lincoln written since World War II, has characterized the proclamation as a document written with "all the moral grandeur of a bill of lading." Many black Americans and radical critics in the 1960s came to believe that Lincoln's heart was not in it, that he was a reluctant emancipator dragged kicking and screaming into the modern age, and—relying on years of revisionist scholarship on this point—that the document really did very little to help black people.[10]

Scholarship at last is turning back to a more realistic appreciation of the Emancipation Proclamation, and the numerous prints issued in Lincoln's day in celebration of the document can help us revive the understanding of that era when the proclamation seemed fresh and genuinely liberating. Even Karl Marx, who thought that all of "Lincoln's Acts appear like the mean pettifogging conditions which one lawyer puts to his opposing lawyer," conceded: "*But this does not alter their historic content. . . .* The events over there are a world upheaval." More representative observers were more enthusiastic. Keeping in mind "the immense opposition ... neutralized or converted by the progress of the war," Emerson admitted that "one can hardly say the deliberation was too long." Lincoln, he added, "has been permitted to do more for America than any other American man." Massachusetts Governor John A. Andrew, who had been critical of the pace of Lincoln's antislavery agenda before the proclamation, afterward hailed it as "a poor *document,* but a mighty *act;* slow, somewhat halting, wrong in its delay till January, but grand and sublime after all." Less radical reformers, like Hannibal Hamlin, Lincoln's Vice-President, simply lauded him for "the great act of the age." The *New York Times* claimed that there was "no more important and far-reaching document ever issued since the foundation of the Government."[11]

It took great events to inspire great portraits. When Lincoln arrived in Washington in 1861, however, few people foresaw the Emancipation Proclamation or a great civil war. If there was any hope that more skillful artists than those who had portrayed him in 1860 would now take advantage of the new President's arrival in the East to renew their attempts to capture his difficult physiognomy, those hopes would soon fade. In Washington, Lincoln would become more readily and regularly available to more people than ever before. Countless people would see him during the first few months of his administration, but relatively few would portray him in any artistic medium.

The great and the near-great, rich and poor, old and new friends, women bearing odd gifts or heartbreaking pleas for pardons, Indians in flamboyant native dress (see Fig. 42), and literary figures from around the world—all these and more, a whole

LINCOLN RECEVANT LES INDIENS COMANCHES.

range of humanity—personally glimpsed Lincoln in Washington
during the first months of his presidency. Many came away surprised at his appearance. The flatterers told him his pictures did
not do him justice; others thought he looked even worse in
person.

The office- and favor-seekers formed a "dense crowd" that
"swarmed in the staircases and corridors . . . the numbers so great
. . . they ceased . . . to be regarded as individuals, drowned as they
were in the general sea of solicitation."[12] Within the mass of
visitors were those who subsequently produced valuable word or
picture portraits of the sixteenth President. But they were the
exception, not the rule.

Hawthorne was one such witness. Interviewing Lincoln in the
White House, he wrote that he was "about the homeliest man I
ever saw," his face "as coarse a one as you would meet anywhere
in the length and breadth of the States," though "brightened" by

"an expression of homely sagacity, that seems weighted with rich results of village experience." Hawthorne included his frank assessment in an article he sent to the *Atlantic Monthly,* but his editors deleted the section on Lincoln. "What a terrible thing it is to try to let off a little bit of truth into this miserable humbug of a world," Hawthorne complained. The author, a Democrat, later confided to correspondent Edward Dicey, "I wish you could have seen Pierce . . . you would have seen a real gentleman."[13]

Walt Whitman saw Lincoln, too, first in New York, en route to his inauguration. To Whitman, Lincoln had a face like "a Hoosier Michael Angelo, so awful ugly it becomes beautiful, with its strange mouth, its deep cut, criss-cross lines, and its doughnut complexion." Whitman worried that "the complete limning of this man's future portrait" would require "four sorts of genius, four mighty and primal hands . . . the eyes and brains and finger-touch of Plutarch and Eschylus and Michael Angelo, assisted by Rabelais."[14]

Whitman would later complain that "no entirely competent and emblematic likeness of Abraham Lincoln in picture or statue" had been created, though he admitted that no "fully appropriate literary statement or summing-up of him" had been produced either—not even by Whitman himself, whose own poetical tributes to the President would not be inspired until the leader had "fallen cold and dead." Having examined dozens of Lincoln portraits, Whitman declared: "I have never seen one yet that in my opinion deserved to be called a perfectly *good likeness.*"[15]

Whitman laid claim to more familiarity with Lincoln than he really had, but even those who saw the President up close tended to the same opinion about his portraits. A soldier who was present when Lincoln toured the encampments of the Army of the

Potomac in Maryland observed: "We had a grand division review . . . in honor of the President who favored us with his presence. My curiosity was gratified by seeing a 'live President,' and, above all, 'Old Abe.' He looks much better than the likeness we see of him—younger, and not so long and lank." Lincoln's secretary, John Nicolay, recalled in 1891 that "there was such a difference between the hard literal shell of the physical man, and the fine ideal fiber . . . of his spirit . . . that no photograph or painting of the former could render even an approximate representation of the latter." He went on to explain:

> Lincoln's features were the despair of every artist who undertook his portrait. The writer saw nearly a dozen, one after another, soon after his first nomination to the presidency, attempt the task. They put into their pictures the large rugged features, and strong prominent lines; they made measurements to obtain exact proportions; they "petrified" some single look, but the picture remained hard and cold. Even before these paintings were finished it was plain to see that they were unsatisfactory to the artists themselves, and much more so to the intimate friends of the man; this was not he who smiled, spoke, laughed, charmed. . . . Graphic art was powerless before a face that moved through a thousand delicate gradations of line and contour, light and shade. . . . There are many pictures of Lincoln; there is no portrait of him.[16]

And yet, the many pictures of Lincoln seem to have provided the American people with more than adequate familiarity with the President's appearance. Satisfying marketplace demand, not the creative ideal, was the imperative that dictated output from the printmakers. By mid-1861, that demand—so far as Lincoln was concerned—seemed sated; few new pictures for the people were produced.

Some engravers, like Thomas Doney and Samuel Sartain, had added beards to update their campaign prints. Currier & Ives and the Kelloggs had done the same to their lithographs. But these were the efforts inspired by post-election public curiosity over Lincoln's new whiskers, not by any interest in maintaining close pictorial scrutiny over Lincoln once his term in office had begun.

Only one known print portrait was issued featuring the words of Lincoln's farewell address to the people of Springfield. Similarly, only one print is known to have featured an "extract from the closing paragraph of Lincoln's Inaugural Message." Surely, the reason was that within a month after his words were spoken, "the better angels of our nature" lay vanquished. When war came, the print—like the speech—was outdated.[17]

Several printmakers issued Lincoln pictures during the first year of his administration. Of these, the earliest typically depicted the new President with his official family. An example of the genre was *Loyal Americans* (Fig. 43) by C. D. Andrews, for which a beardless photograph of Lincoln was updated with uncharacteristically angular whiskers and made the central portrait within a design of smaller medallion likenesses of administration celebrities. Included were portraits of cabinet members, General in Chief Winfield Scott, and three of the early military notables on the Union side. One was Benjamin F. Butler, who seized Baltimore in early 1861 to prevent Maryland from seceding and quickly became one of the most controversial figures in the North and one of the most reviled in the South. Another, Major Robert Anderson, was the commander of Fort Sumter, which fell in April

LOYAL AMERICANS.

Published by B.B. Russell, 515 Wash.? St. Boston.

1861. He appeared frequently in the earliest of Civil War prints, but soon faded into relative obscurity.

Finally, the print depicted Colonel Elmer Ephraim Ellsworth, another familiar figure in these early Civil War portraits. Ellsworth, a twenty-five-year-old onetime student in the Lincoln-Herndon law offices, was killed on May 24, 1861, while on a military patrol, after removing from the roof of an Alexandria, Virginia, hotel a Confederate flag that had been visible all the way to the White House. Lincoln regarded the death as a crushing affliction. To Ellsworth's parents he wrote the first of his famous wartime condolence letters, lamenting the loss of "so much of promised usefulness to one's country, and of bright hopes for one's self and friends. . . ."[18]

Thanks in part to Lincoln, who allowed Ellsworth's body to lie in state in the East Room of the White House, the young officer was quickly elevated to martyr status and mourned throughout the North as the first casualty of the Civil War. As such he was not only included in several Lincoln prints of the period but portrayed in some fifty-two prints and twelve repeatedly reproduced photographs of the young hero himself—a number at least as great as the number of likenesses issued during the same period of the newly installed President of the United States.[19]

Kimmel & Forster's *Outbreak of the Rebellion in the United States, 1861* (Fig. 41) did depict Lincoln in a complicated symbolic tapestry designed to illustrate several of the political and economic factors that provoked the beginning of the war. Here, however, Lincoln owed his prominence in the group portrait to the lithograph's late date of publication, not 1861 but 1865, after the successful conclusion of the war and after Lincoln's assassination and martyrdom.

FIGURE 43. C. D. Andrews after a drawing by A. K. Kipps, *Loyal Americans*, published by B[enjamin]. B. Russell, Boston (*c.* 1861). Lithograph, 8 ⅛ × 9 ¾ in. The medallion portrait of Lincoln is based on the old 1858 Christopher S. German photograph (Fig. 27), with a beard superimposed to bring it up to date. (*Louis A. Warren Lincoln Library and Museum*)

The new military heroes began to be portrayed with greater frequency than the familiar political heroes. Lincoln was the quintessential civilian. It was the Emancipation Proclamation that finally elevated him to an exalted rank he had never before enjoyed, a status that was quickly reflected in engravings and lithographs. As Pennsylvania Governor Andrew G. Curtin put it: "The great proclamation of Liberty will lift the Ruler who uttered it, our Nation, and our age, above all vulgar destiny."[20] As the victim of an assassin, shot on Good Friday, ultimately Lincoln would be compared to Jesus Christ. But now came the first of these mythical analogies: Lincoln was a modern Moses (see Fig. 48). In a volume entitled *Poetical Tributes* published soon after the assassination, half the poems portrayed Lincoln as a Great Emancipator:

> *Our Moses he—whose faithful hand*
> *Led us so near the promised land:*
> *He saw its distant palm trees wave—*

And it was as if

> *The prayer of the bondsman went up night and day,*
> *"Lord, send us a Moses to show us the way."*
> *Like Moses of old, thou didst lead them safe through,*
> *Till the fair land of Canaan each pilgrim could view.*[21]

Before the poets and other writers had begun the process of mythmaking, the printmakers had laid the framework for its acceptance, with a body of Great Emancipator portraiture that circulated throughout the North during Lincoln's lifetime. It was not that the engravers and lithographers more quickly and uniformly converted to abolitionism. Rather, the outpouring of images represented a simple business response to a change in marketplace conditions—the sudden demand from that portion of the public that enthusiastically supported emancipation for timely and understandable visualizations of a significant change in national policy.

Emancipation prints, so called, would fill a great national void. The growing population of photographers in America was dramatic evidence of the considerable public appetite for pictures.[22] But photographs in that day could not depict Lincoln actually signing his great document, nor would any photographs ever capture the President with black people. Printmakers, using both imagination and artistic license, could create the fanciful scenes for which Lincoln himself never sat and the symbolic ones for which he could not sit.

Painters, of course, could create even more heroic portraiture; but their audience was traditionally limited to the very wealthy who could afford to commission such canvases or the relatively few who would subsequently view the efforts at galleries or special exhibits. Hence prints satisfied the national hunger for evocative Emancipation commemoratives that depicted Lincoln heroically and were readily available to the public. Charles Eberstadt, who made a study of Emancipation prints, found twenty-six produced in 1863 and 1864 alone, and he counted only those that reproduced the text of the proclamation. The survival of that many examples is proof positive that Emancipation prints were widely produced and broadly circulated.

Many of the first printed Emancipation tributes were reproductions of the handwritten document itself. Often, they lacked even the most rudimentary portraiture, although some variations on the theme did boast emblematic likenesses of Lincoln. An occasional broadside, such as Martin & Judson's 1864 lithograph, published in Milwaukee, featured matching "slave" and "freedom" scenes (stolen in large part from Thomas Nast's "Emancipation" woodcut in *Harper's Weekly,* January 24, 1863) in addition to the central, flag-ensconced portrait of the Emancipator.[23]

Another way in which publishers of the period drew more direct connection between the proclamation and its author was in the "art" of calligraphy, in which a likeness could be reproduced within a long text by writing certain words in bold relief, together forming an outline portrait within the decorative penmanship. Lincoln had been portrayed in calligraphy before, in a lost print drawn by an artist named David Davidson for the 1860 presidential campaign. A copy was presented to Lincoln that December. Earlier in the month the Boston *Globe* had inspected the picture, marveling over Davidson's use of the text of one of Lincoln's 1858 replies to Douglas in debate, "every word of which he has wrought into hair, eyes, facial lines, shadows, cravat, shirt studs, watch guard, drapery," offering "more flowers of speech than ever its author dreamed of imparting to it." Noted the *Globe:* "Every mark, though microscopically small, has its meaning, and if looked at through a glass the continuity of the speech is easily traced."[24]

The Emancipation Proclamation proved a natural inspiration for calligraphic portraiture, and a number of these novel tributes were published. Peter S. Duval, of Philadelphia, put out two of the more original efforts (see Figs. 44, 46). He was a medal-winning innovator, "the city's principal operator" of "the lithographic press," and one of the country's earliest practitioners of both

FIGURE 44. P[eter]. S. Duval & Son after a drawing by R. Morris Swander, *Emancipation Proclamations./Allegorical Portrait of/Abraham Lincoln./Respectfully dedicated to the Union Leagues of the United States by the Publishers,* published by the Art Publishing Association of Philadelphia, Swander Bishop & Co. (1865). Lithograph 15 ⅞ × 21 in. This calligraphic portrait of Lincoln, formed by the words of the Emancipation Proclamation, featured what might be called "before and after" allegorical border vignettes: to the left, the black man in 1860, a slave being whipped; to the right, the black man in 1865, freed by Columbia and her troops, dressed in frock coat and tie. The outline portrait of Lincoln was based on a Brady studio photograph (Fig. 45). *(Louis A. Warren Lincoln Library and Museum)*

Emancipation Proclamations.

Allegorical Portrait of

ABRAHAM LINCOLN.

Respectfully dedicated to the Union Leagues of the United States by the Publishers
Published by the Art Publishing Association of Philadelphia, Alexander Bishop & Co.

chromolithography and steam-powered printing. "For finish and richness of color," commented the *Bulletin* of the American Art-Union, his output by 1850 rivaled "the best European work." Duval specialized in "all kinds of fancy and ornamental printing," according to his early business cards, and his calligraphic Emancipation prints bore out his claim.[25]

In one of these works, a richly colored full-figure portrait of Lincoln predominated, surrounded by the beautifully transcribed text of the proclamation. It was in fact a reworked design used first by Russell in 1856 for a print of the Declaration of Independence with George Washington as the central figure.[26] Duval's other effort was a more traditional calligraphic portrait, with a familiar likeness of Lincoln made to emerge from within the text of the proclamation, surrounded by ambitious allegorical portraiture in the margins.

Lincoln himself knew of such works. An eyewitness—the artist Francis B. Carpenter, then working on his own pictorial tribute to Emancipation—recalled being asked by a visitor to help arrange an interview with the President "for the purpose of presenting him with an elaborate pen-and-ink 'allegorical, symbolic' representation" of the document, "which, in a massive carved frame, had been purchased at a recent 'Sanitary Fair,' in one of the large cities, by a committee of gentlemen, expressly for this object." Carpenter wrote of the print, now also lost:

> The composition contained a tree, representing Liberty; a portrait of Mr. Lincoln; soldiers, monitors, broken fetters, etc.; together with the text of the proclamation, all executed with a pen. Artistically speaking, such works have no value,—they are simply interesting, as curiosities. Mr. Lincoln kindly accorded the desired opportunity to make the presentation, which occupied but a few

FIGURE 45. Photograph by Anthony Berger at Brady's studios, Washington, D.C. (February 9, 1864). One of the most popular of all photographic models for print portraits of Lincoln, this picture was taken for Francis B. Carpenter as a model for his Emancipation painting. Lincoln's son Robert later judged it "the most satisfactory likeness" of his father. (Hamilton and Ostendorf, *Lincoln in Photographs*, pp. 176–177). The photograph is chiefly familiar to America as the model for the engraving on the five-dollar bill. (*Louis A. Warren Lincoln Library and Museum*)

PRESIDENT LINCOLN AND SECRETARY SEWARD SIGNING
THE PROCLAMATION OF FREEDOM
JANUARY 1ST 1863.
"Upon this act, I invoke the considerate judgment of mankind, and the gracious favor of Almighty God."

FIGURE 46. P[eter]. S. Duval & Son, *Emancipation Proclamation/Issued January 1st, 1863,* published by Gilman R. Russell, Philadelphia (1865). Colored lithograph, 17 ¼ × 25 ½ in. The Lincoln portrait was based on yet another Brady photograph taken at the sitting of February 9, 1864 (see Fig. 70). *(Louis A. Warren Lincoln Library and Museum)*

FIGURE 47. Currier & Ives, *President Lincoln and Secretary Seward Signing/The Proclamation of Freedom/January 1st 1863,* New York (1865). Hand-colored lithograph, 9 ¾ × 12 in. William H. Seward was thought by many to be the power behind the Lincoln throne, and only that erroneous belief explains his prominence in this print. In truth, Seward was responsible for delaying the issuing of the Emancipation

Proclamation until after the North won a battlefield victory. The print included in its caption the peroration of the Emancipation document: "Upon this act, I invoke the considerate judgement of mankind, and the gracious favor of Almighty God"—words suggeested to Lincoln by Secretary of the Treasury Salmon P. Chase. *(Louis A. Warren Lincoln Library and Museum)*

FIGURE 48. Currier & Ives, *Freedom to the Slaves/Proclaimed January 1st 1863, by Abraham Lincoln, President of the United States./"Proclaim liberty throughout All the land unto All the inhabitants thereof."—Lev. XXV, 10,* New York (c. 1865). Lithograph, 8 ¾ × 11 ¾ in. In this simplistic, sentimental scene by Currier & Ives, Lincoln appears to have broken the shackles of the black man kneeling to kiss his outstretched hand, as the freedman's wife and child look on. The print was clearly designed to portray Lincoln as a modern Moses. The quotation in the caption was taken from God's instructions to Moses on Mount Sinai, to greet the liberation with "jubilee," and "return every man united to his family," which is precisely what Lincoln appears to be doing. Lincoln's portrait was based on the Brady studio five-dollar-bill photograph (Fig. 45). *(Louis A. Warren Lincoln Library and Museum)*

moments, and was in the usual form. He accepted the testimonial, he said, not for himself, but in behalf of "the cause in which all were engaged." When the group dispersed, I remained with the President. He returned to his desk; while I examined curiously the pen work, which was exceedingly minute in detail. "This is quite wonderful!" I said, at length. Mr. Lincoln looked up from his papers. "Yes," he rejoined; "it is what I call *ingenious nonsense!*"[27]

There would be further tributes, less ingenious but also less nonsensical, as more and more printmakers came to the understanding that the proclamation was indeed newsworthy. Currier & Ives issued a number of Emancipation tributes: a stiff and awkward depiction (Fig. 47) of Lincoln and Seward signing the document, along with a totally different concept, an imaginary scene (Fig. 48) portraying Lincoln together with a newly freed slave and his family, the slave kneeling at the President's feet as Lincoln gestures grandly toward the heavens. The lithograph was available in a slightly altered state from Currier & Ives, and also in a thinly disguised variant issued by a rival printmaker. In this case, however, with neither version clearly the more polished artistically, it remains difficult to tell which came first and who copied whom.

Some printmakers' reliance on photographic sources remained all but absolute. But as had been the case some years before, during the presidential campaign, prints based on paintings began appearing as well (Figs. 49, 50). Artists soon made their way to the White House to create original studies from which Emancipation engravings and lithographs could be produced.

One painter, Edward Dalton Marchant (1806–1887), arrived

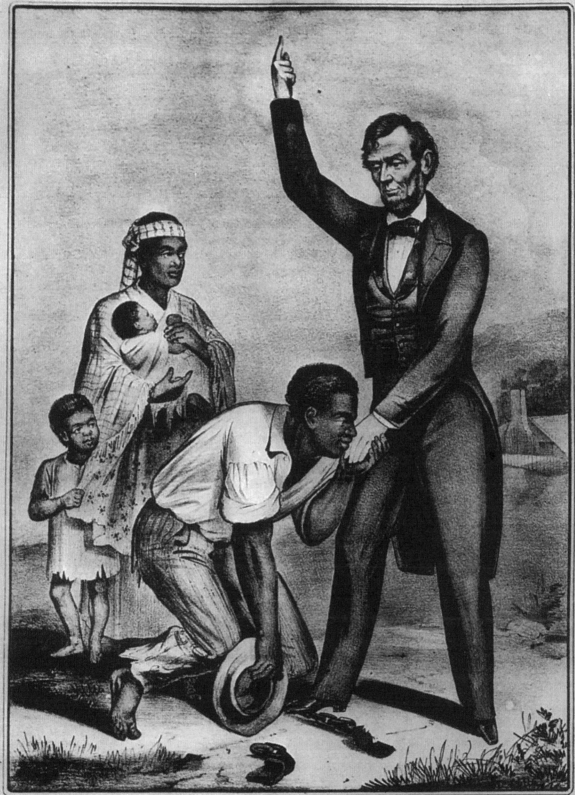

FREEDOM TO THE SLAVES.

Proclaimed January 1st 1863, by ABRAHAM LINCOLN, President of the United States.

"PROCLAIM LIBERTY THROUGHOUT ALL THE LAND UNTO ALL THE INHABITANTS THEREOF." Lev. XXV. 10.

FIGURE 49. David Gilmour Blythe (1815–1865), *Abraham Lincoln Writing the Emancipation Proclamation*, (1863). Oil on canvas, 21 ¾ × 27 ½ in. *(Museum of Art, Carnegie Institute)*

early in 1863, having been commissioned by the President's "personal and political friends" in Philadelphia to paint a commemorative portrait to hang in Independence Hall. Lincoln had paused in Philadelphia en route to the capital for his inauguration in February 1861 to take part in Washington's Birthday ceremonies at the hallowed little building. Raising the flag there, he had pledged to keep it flying over a free and united country. "I would rather be assassinated on this spot," he had declared, "than to surrender it."[28] Now that Lincoln had issued his Emancipation Proclamation, widely regarded as a second Declaration of Independence, the plan was to hang his portrait alongside those of the founding fathers in the very building where the American Union had been formed.

The artist commissioned by the Philadelphia Republicans seemed well suited for the assignment. Marchant, then fifty-six

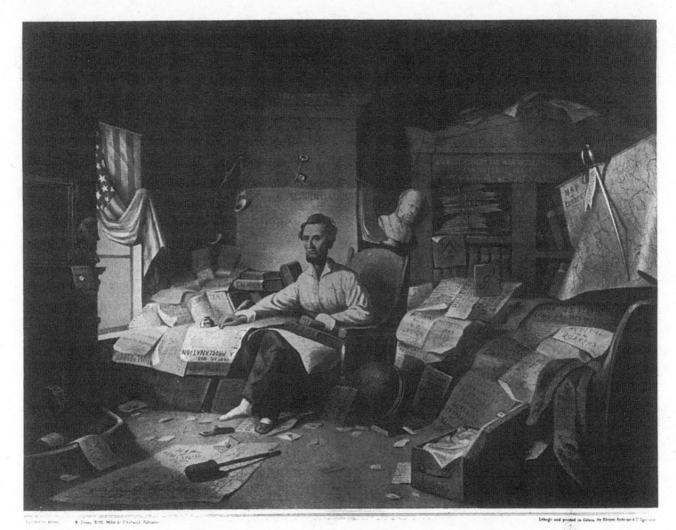

PRESIDENT LINCOLN, WRITING THE PROCLAMATION OF FREEDOM,
January 1ST 1863.

FIGURE 50. [Peter E.] Ehrgott, [Adolphus] Forbriger & Co., after a painting by David Gilmour Blythe, *President Lincoln, Writing the Proclamation of Freedom,/January 1st.1863.* Published in Pittsburgh by M. Dupuy (1864). Chromolithograph, 18 ¼ × 14 ¼ in. The extreme rarity of these prints today suggests that Ehrgott & Forbriger's enthusiasm for Blythe's complex original was not shared by the audience for lithographs at that time. The rampant and overlapping symbolism, including the bust of Buchanan strung by the neck, was aimed ultimately at suggesting that Lincoln's proclamation was firmly rooted in the Bible and the Constitution. Prominent among the artistic devices is the railsplitter's maul in the foreground, carrying with it the implied assurance that Lincoln operated under the important influence of the common man's touch. Lincoln did not write the Proclamation on January 1, 1863, as the caption says; on that day he merely signed the final copy, and it took effect. The Masonic emblem hanging from the bookcase was a reflection of Blythe's own affiliation with Masonry, not President Lincoln's. (Bruce W. Chambers, *The World of David Gilmour Blythe,* Washington, D.C.: Smithsonian Institution Press, 1980, p. 92.) *(Louis A. Warren Lincoln Library and Museum)*

years old, was a native of Edgartown, Massachusetts, and had exhibited at the National Academy of Design as early as 1832. The peripatetic painter moved on to New Orleans, Ohio, New York, Nashville, back to New Orleans, and again to New York, before settling permanently in Philadelphia in 1854.[29]

An important Philadelphia newspaper publisher, John W. Forney, wrote a letter of introduction for Marchant to carry to the President:

> My dear Mr. President—the bearer, Mr. E. D. Marchant, the eminent Artist, has been empowered by a large body of your personal and political friends to paint your picture for the Hall of American Independence. A generous subscription is made—and he visits you to ask your acquiescence, and to exhibit his testimonials. He will need little of your time. There is no likeness of you at Independence Hall. It should be there; and as Mr. Marchant is a most distinguished Artist, and is commanded by the most powerful influences, I trust you will give him a favorable reception.[30]

Lincoln not only agreed to sit for Marchant; he also consented to order a leave of absence for the artist's son, a captain in General Joseph Hooker's army, so that the young man could "consult" on the project. On February 27, 1863, as the time agreed upon for the life sittings drew near, Lincoln wrote to Hooker: "If it will be no detriment to the service I will be obliged for Capt. Henry A. Marchant of Company I, 23rd. Pennsylvania Vols, to come here, to remain four or five days." Young Marchant was released, arrived at the White House, and commenced his "consultation." When the work dragged on longer than anticipated, the President wrote a second letter to Hooker to secure an extension of Henry's leave, "for business purposes, hoping that it

FIGURE 51. Portrait from life by
Edward Dalton Marchant,
Washington, D.C., signed and dated:
E D Marchant./From Life. 1863. Oil
on canvas, 55 × 45 in. Note the
symbolic reference to Emancipation
in the shattered manacles beneath a
barely visible portion of the Liberty
statue at right. The painting now
hangs in Philadelphia's Union League
Club. (*The Art Collection of The Union
League of Philadelphia*)

ABRAHAM LINCOLN.

Abraham Lincoln

FIGURE 52. John Sartain, after a painting by Edward Dalton Marchant, *Abraham Lincoln,/16th President of the United States* (with facsimile signature: *Abraham Lincoln*), published by Bradley & Co., Philadelphia (1864). Engraving, 10 × 13 in. The engraving faithfully copied the Marchant original, except in the spelling on the Liberty statue at right. The references to the Emancipation Proclamation are understated but a little less so than in the painting. The writing is now visible on the document, for example, which appears to represent the proclamation. This may be the only print portrait of Abraham Lincoln in white tie. *(Library of Congress)*

will not interfere with the public service."[31] Young Marchant, just twenty-four years old, had himself been a minor painter of miniatures, possibly taught by his father, and while he was probably not essential to the creation of the Lincoln canvas, his father no doubt craved a reunion.

"My studio was for several months in the White House," Marchant recalled years later, "where I was in daily communication with the remarkable man whose features I sought to portray." Marchant characterized his effort as "more truly a labor of love than I am often permitted to perform." Writing some time later to fellow artist Daniel Huntington, Marchant said of Lincoln, "He was seldom twice alike. Hence the endless variety observable in the photographs we have of him." As for Lincoln's features,

FIGURE 53. Henry Sartain after his own ambrotype, *John Sartain* (facsimile signature; date unknown). Sartain's was the premier printmaking family in America, as this engraving by his son indicates. The elder Sartain lived nearly ninety years and saw three of his sons—Henry, Samuel, and William—become prominent printmakers. *(Chicago Historical Society)*

FIGURE 54. Group portrait from life by Francis Bicknell Carpenter, *First Reading of the Emancipation Proclamation of President Lincoln,* Washington, D.C. (1864). Oil on canvas, 15 ft × 9 ft. 2 in. Lincoln's last attorney general, James Speed, called this a "great picture," and told the artist: "You have not sunk the natural in the heroic, a fault so common that it must be difficult for an artist to avoid it." The *New York Evening Post* believed that Carpenter had "achieved a success which time will go on ripening to the latest day that Americans honor the nobility of their ancestors" (quoted in advertising endpapers, pp. 6–7, of Francis B. Carpenter, *Six Months at The White House With Abraham Lincoln. The Story of a Picture.* New York: Hurd & Houghton, 1867). (U.S. Capitol photograph)

Marchant confessed, "Though indelibly impressed upon my mind during a residence of four months at the White House, they are the most difficult to describe that I ever knew," making Lincoln "the most difficult subject who ever taxed" his skills as an artist.[32]

Marchant's portrait (Fig. 51) was exhibited only briefly in Independence Hall. The engraved adaptation (Fig. 52) by John Sartain (Fig. 53) appeared in 1864, and its caption indicated that the original was already "in the possession of the Union League of Philadelphia," where it remains today. A little-known second painting by Marchant was done at the White House at Lincoln's request as a gift for William Whiting. Whiting was the War Department solicitor who had argued in a famous work, *War Powers of the President,* that Lincoln was entitled to the extraordinary executive authority necessary to issue the Emancipation Proclamation.[33]

Marchant claimed he had enjoyed "daily communications" with Lincoln for "several months," but without a doubt, no artist was afforded a better or more protracted opportunity to portray the sixteenth President than Francis Bicknell Carpenter (1830–1900; Fig. 55). A New York painter who had already completed portraits of two American presidents, Carpenter spent six months

KEY TO THE PICTURE

THE MEN

1. PRESIDENT LINCOLN.
2. WILLIAM H. SEWARD, Secretary of State.
3. SALMON P. CHASE, Secretary of Treasury.
4. EDWIN M. STANTON, Secretary of War.
5. GIDEON WELLES, Secretary of Navy.
6. EDWARD BATES, Attorney-General.
7. MONTGOMERY BLAIR, Postmaster-General.
8. CALEB B. SMITH, Secretary of Interior.

The room is the Official Chamber of the White House, in which all Cabinet meetings are held, and in which the President receives calls upon official business.

ACCESSORIES

9. Photograph of Simon Cameron, Ex-Sec. War.
10. Portrait of Andrew Jackson.
11. Parchment Copy of the Constitution.
12. Map of Seat of War in Virginia.
13. Map showing Slave Population in gradulight and shade.
14. War Department Portfolio.
15. Story's "Commentaries on the Constitution."
16. Whiting's "War Powers of the President."
17. New York *Tribune*.
18. Two volumes *Congressional Globe*.

FIGURE 55. Photograph of Francis B. Carpenter, taken April 26, 1864, in which the famous painter assumes the pose in which he would later paint William H. Seward in his Emancipation painting (Fig. 54). The picture was taken by a Brady studio camera operator in the White House cabinet room, where Lincoln himself also posed for several photographs at the artist's request. *(Louis A. Warren Lincoln Library and Museum)*

at the White House, from February through July 1864, working on a life-sized portrayal of the first reading of the proclamation before the cabinet. The famous painting, which now hangs in the U.S. Capitol, was pronounced by contemporary critics an "unrivaled masterpiece of American historical painting . . . which, by universal consent, has placed Mr. Carpenter's name second to none on the roll of eminent modern artists." Later, art historians sharply downgraded Carpenter's reputation; but at the time he provided the nation with the historical painting the critics so wanted to see come out of the Civil War.[34]

During his long stay, through most of which he made the state dining room his studio, Carpenter produced life sketches of Lincoln and studies of all the cabinet secretaries he would portray (except for Caleb B. Smith, who had died), created a number of smaller canvases of Lincoln and his family, commissioned special photographs (see Fig. 56) for use as models, and, in general, functioned almost as an official artist-in-residence.

What makes Carpenter's work remarkable is, principally, the special status he enjoyed inside the White House while creating it. Lincoln's acquiescence in the project strongly suggests that whatever personal humility, embarrassment about his appearance, or "indifference" over the fine arts he may have felt, the President was also keenly aware of the importance of Emancipation. He was willing to devote much time to the creation of a heroic portrait to immortalize it. Knowing that he "could not escape history," Lincoln did his part to make sure that the historical record was complete in graphic terms, too.

The story of Carpenter's labors is the story of a large vision, couched though it was in terms of naivete, sentiment, and hero worship. The story of his painting's timely and skillful adaptation as a popular print is one of unusual enterprise and skill on the part of an engraver as well. In the end, if Carpenter did not have quite enough talent to carry off his ambition, he did possess the prescience to keep a written record of his White House stay. His is the only extended memoir that we have from an artist involved with Lincoln.

Carpenter, born in 1830 on a farm near Homer, in upstate New York, had been a portrait painter for most of his young life, the proprietor of a New York studio by his twenty-first birthday. He had already painted Millard Fillmore and Franklin Pierce but now found himself particularly inspired by the Emancipation Proclamation—"an act unparalleled for moral grandeur in the history of mankind." To Carpenter, the proclamation meant that the war "had assumed the form of a direct issue between Freedom and Slavery."[35]

"To paint a picture which should commemorate this new epoch in the history of Liberty," he wrote, "was a dream which took form and shape in my mind towards the close of the year 1863," when he was gripped by "an intense desire to do something expressive of . . . the great issues involved in the war." In his 1866 memoir, *Six Months at the White House,* the artist recounted in revealing detail the subsequent plan and execution of his painting. Its genesis was traced to Carpenter's analysis of Emancipation itself. "The long-prayed-for year of jubilee had come," he wrote, "the bonds of the oppressed were loosed; the prison doors were opened. 'Behold,' said a voice, 'how a Man may be exalted to a dignity and glory almost divine, and give freedom to a race. Surely Art should unite with Eloquence and Poetry to celebrate such a theme.'" Eloquence did not necessarily call for artistic allegory. Indeed, Carpenter believed that the proclamation was "no dream of fable, but a substantial fact—the immaculate conception of Constitutional Liberty."[36]

Carpenter thought a "realistic" approach would be most appropriate. Since the proclamation "was . . . second only in historical importance . . . to the Declaration of Independence," if "honestly and earnestly painted, it need borrow no interest from imaginary curtain or column, gorgeous furniture or allegorical statue. Assenting heartily to what is called the 'realistic' school of art, when applied to the illustration of historic events, I felt in this case that I had no more right to depart from the facts, than has the historian in his record." Carpenter's credo was clearly stated on the very first page of his book. "That Art should aim to embody and express the spirit and best thought of its own age seems self-evident," he wrote. "If it fails to do this, whatever else it may accomplish, it falls short of its highest object. It cannot dwell always among classic forms, nor clothe its conceptions in the imagery of an old and worn-out world. It must move on. . . ."

And he vowed: "If I cannot make the portraiture of the scene itself sufficiently attractive without the false glitter of tapestry hangings, velvet table-cloths, and marble columns, then I shall at least have the satisfaction of having failed in the cause of truth."[37]

The realistic approach decided upon, Carpenter next began groping for a specific blueprint for the painting. One night, seized by inspiration, he grabbed a loose photograph in his room and on the back "roughly and hastily sketched . . . the central idea of the composition as it had shaped itself" in his mind. He would portray not the writing of the proclamation, not the signing of it into law, and not its direct effect on black Americans. Instead:

> I conceived of that band of men, upon whom the eyes of the world centred as never before upon ministers of state, gathered in council, depressed, perhaps disheartened at the vain efforts of many months to restore the supremacy of the government. I saw . . . the head of the nation, bowed down with his weight of care and responsibility, solemnly announcing, as he unfolded the prepared draft of the Proclamation, that the time for the inauguration of this policy had arrived; I endeavored to imagine the conflicting emotions of satisfaction, doubt, and distrust with which such an announcement would be received by men of the varied characteristics of the assembled councillors.[38]

It would be a painting, then, of the first reading of the proclamation to the cabinet. Now Carpenter had to find two benefactors: one to sponsor him financially, the other to introduce him to the President and pave the way for him to secure sittings. Frederick A. Lane appeared, as if "sent" by fate, Carpenter later recalled, and agreed to provide the necessary money. In January 1864, Carpenter wrote to Illinois Congressman Owen Lovejoy, the brother of the martyred abolitionist Elijah Lovejoy, to ask him to recommend the project to Lincoln.

"I never felt a stronger . . . assurance of success in any undertaking in my life," Carpenter wrote to Lovejoy. "I wish to paint this picture *now* while all the actors in the scene are living and while they are still in the discharge of the duties of their several high offices—I wish to make it the *standard* authority for the portrait of each and all especially *Mr. Lincoln* as it is the great act of his life by which he will be remembered and honored through all generations!" He reiterated his conviction that "most historical pictures (so called) are merely the fancy pieces of their authors. [John] Ruskin the great modern thinker and writer on art says that the *portrait* is the only *true* historical picture!" Finally, Carpenter asked Lovejoy to secure for him "the facilities which can only be afforded me at the 'White House,' " adding: "will you have the kindness my dear sir, to lay this note before the President. . . ?" Carpenter promised that not only would the finished canvas be "exhibited in all the leading cities of the loyal states," but "a steel engraving in the highest style will be made in England from a small copy I shall make of the large picture."[39]

Although critically ill at the time (he died on March 25), Lovejoy apparently helped win Carpenter a favorable reaction from Lincoln. The artist rushed to Washington and went to a White House reception. There, for the first time he saw a "haggard-looking" President, "solitary and alone" even in a crowd of well-wishers whose greetings were unable to alter the expression on the "saddest face" Carpenter had ever seen. The artist remembered "the electric thrill which went through my whole being" at this first glimpse of Abraham Lincoln. Before long, Carpenter presented himself to the President, and Lincoln greeted him in a voice "so loud as to attract the attention of those in immediate proximity." Laughed Lincoln: "Do you think, Mr. C——, that you can make a handsome picture of *me*?"[40]

Later that evening, Carpenter pressed his case at a private meeting in Lincoln's office. The President read Lovejoy's endorsement and, taking off his glasses, turned to the artist and said: "Well, Mr. C——, we will turn you in loose here, and try to give you a good chance to work out your idea." Lincoln proved unusually helpful. He recounted for Carpenter his own recollections of the events that led up to the writing and reading of the proclamation, and then led the painter on a guided tour of the cabinet room, where he pointed out the precise places his secretaries had occupied the day he had read to them his document. The "republican simplicity of the room and furniture," Carpenter felt, "with its thronging associations," would more than make up for "the lack of splendor." As for the general arrangement of the group, Carpenter found Lincoln's placement of his secretaries "fortunately entirely consistent with my purpose, which was to give that prominence to the different individuals which belonged to them respectively in the Administration." Something subtly symbolic, within the realistic framework Carpenter had plotted, was taking shape in his thoughts:

There was a curious mingling of fact and allegory in my mind, as I assigned to each his place on the canvas. There were two elements in the Cabinet, the radical and the conservative. Mr. Lincoln was placed at the head of the official table, between two groups, nearest that representing the radical, but the uniting point of both. The chief powers of a government are War and Finance: the ministers of these were at his right—the Secretary of War, symbolizing the great struggle, in the immediate foreground; the Secretary of the Treasury, actively supporting the new policy, standing by the President's side. . . . To the Secretary of State, as the great expounder of the principles of the Republican party . . . would the attention of all at such a time be given. . . . The . . . chief officers of the government were thus brought, in accordance with their relations to the Administration, nearest the person of the President, who, with the manuscript proclamation in hand, which he had just read, was represented leaning forward, listening to, and intently considering the views presented by the Secretary of State.

This is the way Carpenter described his final design to its principal subject, and it proves that by "historical" and "factual" he meant "not neoclassical"; there was still plenty of room for art. "It is as good as it can be made," Carpenter recalled Lincoln commenting, when the artist first sketched it out on the huge ten-foot by fifteen-foot canvas assembled on an easel in the state dining room.[41]

From that moment forward, the artist's enthusiasm "flagged not to the end." Carpenter often worked throughout the night, unaware of time, until "the morning light" shone in, finding the artist "still standing pencil or palette in hand, before the immense canvas, unable to break the spell which bound me to it."[42]

When William H. Seward saw the finished painting later, he scoffed at Carpenter's choice of the Emancipation Proclamation as "the great feature of the Administration." To the Secretary of State, the antislavery acts of the administration were "merely incidental"; its great work was the preservation of the Union and through that "the saving of popular government for the world." Carpenter would have done better to go back to the grim cabinet

FIGURE 56. Photograph by a camera
operator from the Brady studios, the
White House, Washington (April 26,
1864). This is one of several poses
requested by Carpenter, most of
them badly lighted by studio
standards and all of them nearly
ruined when Lincoln's son absconded
with the darkroom key. (*Louis A.
Warren Lincoln Library and Museum*)

meeting following the Baltimore massacre when the administration invoked extraordinary war powers to meet the crisis, performing "acts that might have brought them all to the scaffold."[43]

A painting that provokes debate among the leaders of the government over the central meaning of their efforts is no mean work of art.[43] Carpenter had a way of sensing the most important currents of his era. Perhaps his ardent antislavery views played a part; he may also have been influenced by his close friendship with the theologian Theodore Thornton Munger and other New England intellectuals. Whatever the explanation, Carpenter's work tended to get to the heart of things and, therefore, to provoke thoughtful responses.

His sketches progressing nicely, Carpenter began gathering the photographs he would need as models for his portraits. On February 9, he accompanied Lincoln to Mathew Brady's gallery for a particularly fruitful sitting—two of the pictures were later engraved for American coins and currency. But Carpenter was not yet satisfied. A Brady camera operator was sent for and took pictures of Lincoln in the White House cabinet room (Fig. 56). Carpenter also began ushering cabinet ministers to the photographers; Secretary of the Navy Gideon Welles, for example, recorded a visit to "Brady's rooms" on February 17.[44]

Carpenter was pleased to be granted "free" access to "the shop"—Lincoln's term for his White House office. There he would sit, "absorbed frequently in a pencil sketch," while the President worked. If a visitor eyed the artist with suspicion, Lincon would cry out: "Oh, you need not mind him; he is but a painter."[45]

Carpenter was awed by Lincoln's demanding routine, both the paperwork and the "public opinion baths," as Lincoln called those occasions when his office was thrown open to visitors and favor-seekers. After only twenty-four hours, the President asked: "Well, Carpenter, you have seen one day's run;—what is your opinion of it?" His opinion was that it seemed more than most mortals could bear. He saw Lincoln physically ejecting offensive guests, calling guards to remove a "saucy" woman, and on other occasions listening to tales of woe that left the President's face imbued "with a sorrow almost divine." He observed: "There were days when I could scarcely look into it without crying . . . such a picture of the effects of sorrow, care, and anxiety as would have melted the hearts of the worst of his adversaries, who so mistakenly applied to him the epithets of tyrant and usurper." On March 2, Carpenter "had an unusually long and interesting sitting from the President," during which Lincoln recited Shakespearean soliloquies from memory. On another day, "by special permission of Mr. Lincoln," Carpenter "was present at the regular Cabinet meeting," where he watched the group in action for the first time.[46]

Before long it was Lincoln who was observing Carpenter, and from time to time "bringing many friends" into the dining room (which the artist now referred to as his "studio") to inspect the picture. Mrs. Lincoln, who spent so much of her time in the White House in mourning, was slowly losing her grip on reality, but Carpenter's painting evoked a momentary display of her old wit. After studying the portraits of the cabinet she so frequently criticized, she dubbed the painting "the happy family." Another touch of humor came via Horace Greeley, who insisted that he preferred the engraved likenesses in his own book, *The American Conflict.* Carpenter attributed the famous journalist's opinion to the fact that Greeley was "very near-sighted."[47]

At the end of "six months' incessant labor," Carpenter's "task at the White House drew near completion." On July 22, Lincoln led the entire cabinet into the state dining room for a final inspection, where the President "expressed his 'unschooled' opinion," Carpenter recalled, ". . . in terms which could not but have afforded the deepest gratification to any artist." Lincoln ordered that the painting (Fig. 54) go on public display in the East Room, which was "thronged with visitors" for the brief exhibition. Then, just before painter and canvas were scheduled to depart, Lincoln told Carpenter: "I must go in and take one more look at the picture before you leave us."[48]

Secretary of the Treasury Salmon P. Chase complained that the "whole picture" was made "subsidiary to Seward who is talking while every one else either listens or stares into vacancy," but Lincoln did not object to Carpenter's placement of the subjects. "There is little to find fault with," the President proclaimed. "The portraiture is the main thing, and that seems to me absolutely perfect." And Lincoln added (or so Carpenter recalled his words): "I am right glad you have done it . . . as affairs have turned, it is the central act of my Administration, and the great event of the nineteenth century."[49]

Appropriately, just as Carpenter had promised Owen Lovejoy seven months earlier, the painting was quickly engraved (Fig. 57), not by an English printmaker, however, but by Alexander Hay Ritchie (1822–1895) a Scottish-born New Yorker. According to a brochure issued for a Boston exhibit of the Carpenter original, the "Great National Painting" was by late 1864 "now being executed" as a "magnificent Steel Plate Engraving." Subscriptions were already being made available, at $50 for signed artist's proofs, $25 for india proofs, and $10 for plain prints. Lincoln

FIGURE 57. Alexander Hay Ritchie after a painting by Francis B. Carpenter, *The First Reading of rhe Emancipation Proclamation Before the Cabinet,* published by Derby & Miller, New York (1864). Engraving, 32 ⅜ × 20 ¾ in. One of the most widely circulated of all the Lincoln prints published during his lifetime, Ritchie's superior adaptation of Carpenter's painting (Fig. 54) was apparently issued before the artist had completed final revisions on his canvas. The portrait of Lincoln in the engraving bears a much closer resemblance to Carpenter's preliminary sketches than to the Lincoln in the finished painting. *The Independent* thought the print "large enough, when hanging on the wall of a room, to show the portraits distinctly at a considerable distance," and The *Evening Post* predicted that the engraving would "take its place among the pictures which the people hang upon their walls to commemorate one of the great and most notable acts in the nation's history" (Carpenter, *Six Months at The White House,* appendix, pp. 8, 5). The engraving was pirated (see Fig. 59), with little regard for the precise and politically symbolic arrangement of the principals in the Carpenter original. *(Gettysburg College)*

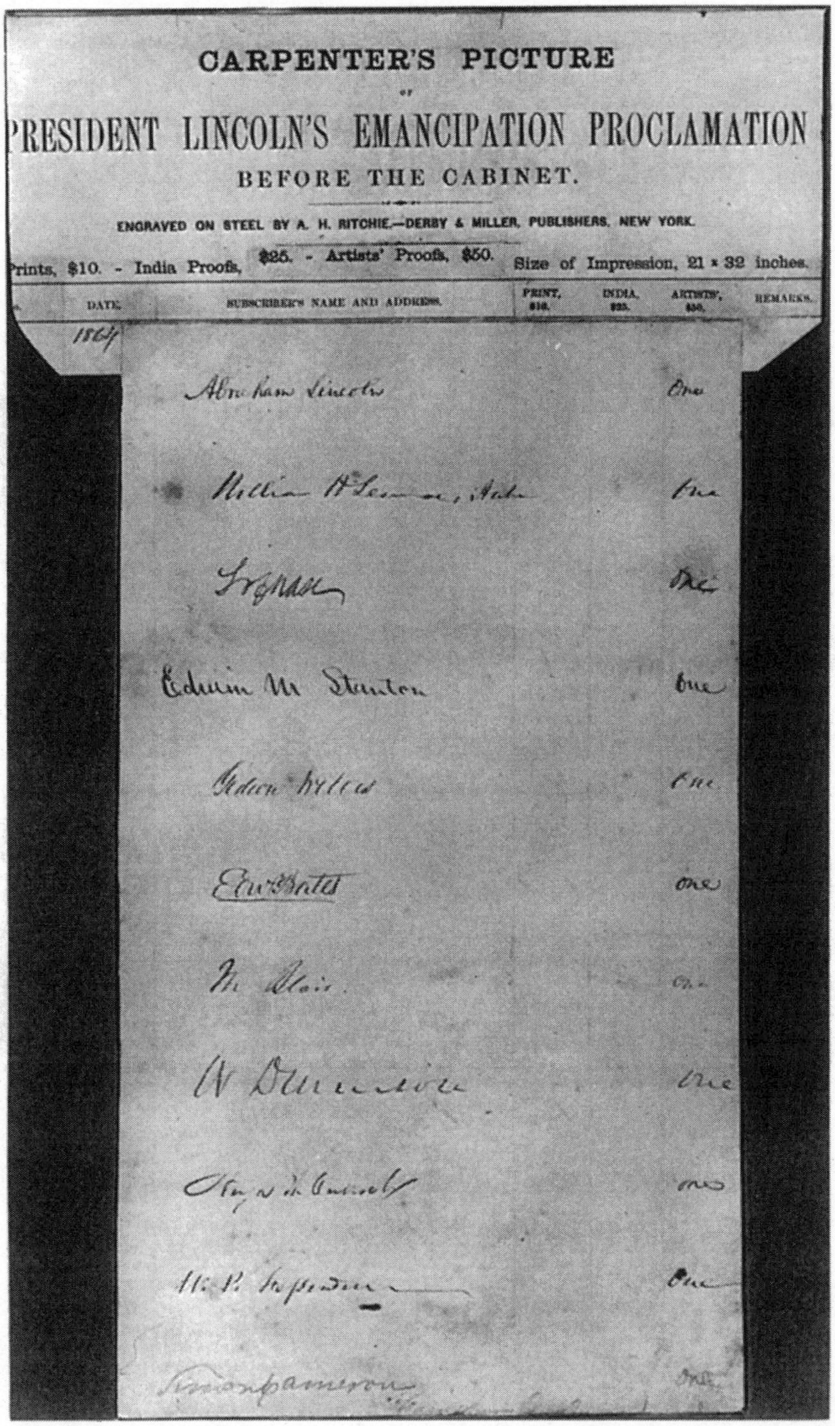

CARPENTER'S PICTURE

OF

'RESIDENT LINCOLN'S EMANCIPATION PROCLAMATION

BEFORE THE CABINET.

ENGRAVED ON STEEL BY A. H. RITCHIE.—DERBY & MILLER, PUBLISHERS, NEW YORK.

rints, $10. - India Proofs, $25. - Artists' Proofs, $50. Size of Impression, 21 x 32 inches.

DATE	SUBSCRIBER'S NAME AND ADDRESS	PRINT, $10.	INDIA, $25.	ARTISTS', $50.	REMARKS.
1864	Abraham Lincoln			One	
	Edwin M Stanton			One	

FIGURE 58. Abraham Lincoln buys a print (1864). Heading a list of buyers that included all the surviving subjects portrayed in Carpenter's Emancipation painting, Lincoln signed on to purchase for $50 an artist's proof of the Ritchie engraving. *(National Portrait Gallery)*

himself signed on as the very first subscriber (see Fig. 58), but at a higher price, $50 for an artist's proof. So did all the other living subjects portrayed in the canvas. If a copy was in fact delivered to the President, then it became the only print portrait of himself that he is ever known to have purchased. Mary Lincoln did receive a copy two years later from Derby & Miller, the New York publishers who issued it. In her acknowledgment, Mary offered this rare endorsement: "I have always regarded the original painting, as

PRESIDENT LINCOLN AND HIS CABINET.   READING OF THE EMANCIPATION PROCLAMATION

FIGURE 59. Edward Herline, *President Lincoln and His Cabinet, Reading of the Emancipation Proclamation*, published by D. Hensel & Co. and Goff & Bros., Philadelphia (1866). Lithograph, 29 ½ × 23 ⅝ in. With some obvious modifications, this is a piracy of Ritchie's engraving (Fig. 57). Among the alterations are these: the portrait of Stanton is reversed and moved to the chair originally occupied by Seward, while Seward is moved to the far side of the cabinet table but in much the same pose; Blair is merely shifted from Smith's left to Chase's left; and a few books are added to the mantel. The portrait of Lincoln is the most original aspect of the Herline print. It appears to be a mirror-image adaptation of the Brady studio's 1864 photograph of Lincoln with Tad (Fig. 82). *(Library of Congress)*

very perfect, and the engraving, appears to me quite equal to it."[50]

The result of Carpenter's close relationship with the Lincoln White House was not only a valuable (if admittedly "rambling and fragmentary") book of reminiscences, but a well-received pictorial tribute to Emancipation, which was exhibited—fulfilling yet another of his pledges to Lovejoy—throughout the country. After a temporary showing in the rotunda of the U.S. Capitol, it was in 1878 purchased from Carpenter for $25,000 by Mrs. Elizabeth Thompson, who donated it to the Capitol's permanent collection.

The portraiture in the Carpenter painting looks markedly different, especially where Lincoln is concerned, from the effect in Ritchie's engraving. Ritchie had worked from the small copy Carpenter created for that purpose, but that painting was subsequently lost in a fire at the artist's studio; there is no way to compare it to the print adaptation. However, Carpenter made many changes in his main canvas over the years, even after its exhibit at the Capitol, some fourteen years after it was painted.[51]

He may have altered the painting once too often. The work in the engraving today seems superior. Moreover, while most prints of famous paintings sought to exploit the popularity of familiar originals, in Carpenter's case Ritchie's engraving probably made the painting popular. As late as 1879, it was being offered as a premium for subscriptions to the newspaper *The Independent.*[52]

The Emancipation Proclamation, of course, had plenty of critics. Among artists in the North, the most notable, daring, and talented of these was Dr. Adalbert Johann Volck (1828–1912) (Fig. 60), a Bavarian-born Copperhead dentist from Baltimore who produced a series of secretly published anti-Union etchings

FIGURE 60. Undated photograph of
Dr. Adalbert Johann Volck by E.
Balch, Baltimore. *(Maryland Historical
Society)*

during the war. He had learned his avocation at an artist's colony
in Nuremberg; his political beliefs he acquired in the slave society
of Maryland. Applying them to art, he became, in the words of a
modern critic, an apologist for all "the values, myths, and fears
that were the psychological underpinnings of the Confederacy."[53]

Volck portrayed Lincoln variously as a man bribing a modern-
day Judas to keep Maryland in the Union, as a harem dancer
concealing behind a veil the fact that he is black, as a puppeteer
manipulating a pathetic band of cabinet-level marionettes, and as
the physical coward who had allegedly slipped through Baltimore
in disguise en route to his inauguration. In one of his most
provocative efforts, Volck portrayed Lincoln *Writing the Emancipa-*

tion Proclamation (Fig. 61): a devilishly inspired villain calling upon a number of historical symbols of presumed evil as muses for the authorship of the hated document. Most printmakers, however, were more celebratory than critical. And their pro-Emancipation prints may have helped create a new Lincoln image by which he could be judged as he sought reelection.

The large body of Emancipation prints helps explain the dearth of new prints issued for the campaign of 1864. However, a number of other factors also account for the rarity of 1864 campaign prints in contrast to the great number issued four years earlier. For one thing, Lincoln had been an unknown in 1860. At that time, pictures were needed to meet a public demand for representations of the dark horse Republican presidential candidate. It was Lincoln's status as a "new face," and not the political dynamics of the election, that triggered the outpouring of images. Printmakers thus responded to market conditions rather than electoral conditions. When Lincoln grew a beard, he created another new face, prompting another unusual production of new prints. The Emancipation Proclamation stimulated yet another unusual outpouring of images. In 1864, Lincoln was a known quantity, a known face, a familiar incumbent running for reelection (the first President to do so since Van Buren). Carpenter published this illustrative anecdote in his memoir: "A visitor, congratulating Mr. Lincoln on the prospects of his reëlection, was answered with an anecdote of an Illinois farmer who undertook to blast his own rocks. His first effort at producing an explosion proved a failure. He explained the cause by exclaiming, 'Pshaw, this powder has been shot before.' "[54] It seems the printmakers agreed that where Lincoln as a subject for popular pictures was concerned, the powder had been shot before.

FIGURE 61. Adalbert Johann Volck [*Writing the Emancipation Proclamation*], Baltimore (*c.* 1864). Etching, 6 ¼ × 4 ⅞ in. The work of a Copperhead who covertly published "War Sketches" under a pseudonym formed by reversing and abbreviating his first name "V. Blada," this etching includes such details as Lincoln using a pen dipped in a devil's inkstand, a wall portrait of a sanctified John Brown, a vulture's head serving as a drapery tie-back, table legs with cloven feet, Liberty with a baboon's head, and a copy of the Constitution being trampled beneath Lincoln's foot. Equally suggestive on a more worldly level is the liquor decanter on the table at right—implying spirits other than humanitarian under which Lincoln is here alleged to have written his proclamation. (*Louis A. Warren Lincoln Library and Museum*)

GRAND, NATIONAL UNION BANNER FOR 1864.

LIBERTY, UNION AND VICTORY.

FIGURE 62. Currier & Ives, *Grand National Union Banner for 1864./Liberty, Union and Victory*, New York (1864). Hand-colored lithograph, 12 × 8 13/16 in. The promise of peace is subtly evoked in this print from the second Lincoln campaign: the accessory portrait beneath those of the candidates represents neither war nor Emancipation but a return to bucolic tranquility, further suggested by a harvest of fruit spilling over from twin cornucopias alongside. As the caption implies, it was a promise possible only through "Union" and "Victory." (*Louis A. Warren Lincoln Library and Museum*)

ABRAHAM LINCOLN.   ANDREW JOHNSON.

PRESIDENT AND VICE-PRESIDENT.

FIGURE 63. E[dmund]. B[urke]. and E[lijah]. C[hapman]. Kellogg, *Abraham Lincoln./Andrew Johnson./President and Vice-President,* Hartford, Connecticut, and New York City, New York (copublished by F. P. Whiting; late 1864 or early 1865). Hand-colored lithograph, 9 × 12 ⅛ in. In this print, land and sea commerce are seen thriving again, the scales of justice are restored to perfect balance, and a pair of cornucopias overflows with wheat, manufactured goods, and armaments. *(Louis A. Warren Lincoln Library and Museum)*

The truth can probably be found in all of these explanations. It is most likely that the absence of much new portraiture was dictated by the continuing availability of existing Lincoln prints. Thus, despite the substitution of a new vice-presidential nominee, Andrew Johnson, and the temporary redesignation of the Republicans as the "Union" party, the centerpiece of the campaign, Lincoln himself, had simply not changed enough to create new public demand for campaign prints.

An occasional poster (Figs. 62, 63) was published, along with a handful of both supportive and sinister caricatured images, several aimed at lampooning Lincoln's reputation for inappropriate humor (Fig. 64), never a real asset in sober Victorian America. Several cartoons (see Fig. 64) seized on Shakespearean themes, reflecting the cartoonists' new piece of information on the old railsplitter: he liked the Bard's plays. A more resolute attempt to circulate anti-Lincoln pictorial propaganda might have had more of an impact on the election, but satire was never the prevailing motif in popular American prints. Sentimentalism dominated national taste—even highbrow taste. And sentiment clearly had increased its dominance over Lincoln art by 1864. Lincoln had now freed the slaves. He was leading a war effort. Art had helped to forge this new Lincoln image; it would be difficult for art to tear it down.

Lincoln received 56 percent of the vote that November, helped in large part by an overwhelming mandate from the separately-counted soldiers' ballots. *Harper's Weekly*, reflecting the unbridled joy of the Republican press, declared the results "the proclamation of the American people that they are not conquered; that the rebellion is not successful; and that, deeply as they deplore war and its inevitable suffering and loss, yet they

"I KNEW HIM, HORATIO; A FELLOW OF INFINITE JEST. * * * WHERE BE YOUR GIBES NOW?—*Hamlet, Act IV., Scene 1.*]

FIGURE 64. J. H. Howard, *"I Knew Him, Horatio; A Fellow of Infinite Jest.*** Where Be Your Gibes Now—Hamlet, Act IV, Scene 1*, probably published by T[homas]. W. Strong, New York (1864). Lithograph, 13 ⅞ × 10 ¼ in. For this striking composition based on the gravediggers' scene of *Hamlet* (which occurs in Act V, Scene 1, not Act IV), Democratic presidential candidate George B. McClellan is the prince of Denmark, and the White House, not Elsinore, looms in the distance. The portrayal of one of the gravediggers, strangely enough, caricatures an Irish immigrant with features normally used in anti-Democratic cartoons. *(Louis A. Warren Lincoln Library and Museum)*

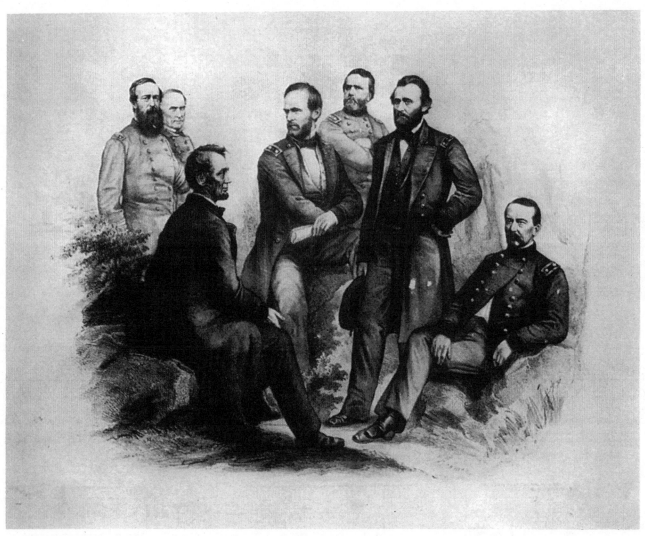

FIGURE 65. P[eter], Kramer, *Lincoln and His Generals.* Printed by A[lphonse]. Brett and published by Jones & Clark, New York, and C. A. Asp, Boston (1865). Lithograph, 19 1/8 × 15 1/8 in. This depiction of a supposed battlefield conference portrays, left to right, Admiral David D. Porter, Admiral David G. Farragut, Lincoln, General William T. Sherman, General George Thomas, General Ulysses S. Grant, and General Philip Sheridan. Its intention was to portray Lincoln as an active, on-site commander in chief, a position which Lincoln had once threatened to assume. This is one of the few prints to portray Lincoln out of his natural milieu, the White House, where, surrounded by the trappings of office, he was the unrivaled chief. Here, the setting is military, and the President sits not in a chair of state but on a rock. Yet even in this exposed environment, and despite his apparent vulnerability, Lincoln is unquestionably the central figure in the scene, the character to whom all eyes are turned. Probably because it was rendered in a highly realistic style, this print was photographed and reissued to resemble an authentic *carte-de-visite* entitled "Lincoln and His Generals In Council Before Richmond." The portrait of Lincoln was modeled after a Brady studio photograph (Fig. 66). (*Library of Congress*)

FIGURE 66. Photograph by the Brady studios, Washington, D.C., February 9, 1864. This pose is chiefly familiar as the model for the engraved portrait on the Lincoln penny. (*Louis A. Warren Lincoln Library and Museum*)

have no choice between war and national ruin, and must therefore fight on." To the Richmond, Virginia, *Dispatch,* on the other hand, the reelection of Lincoln meant that "twenty millions of human beings" had made "a formal surrender of their liberties ... to a vulgar tyrant, who has ... no more idea of statesmanship than as a means of making money; whose career has been one of unlimited and unmitigated disaster; whose personal qualities are those of a low buffoon, and whose most note-worthy conversation is a medley of profane jests and obscene anecdotes."[55]

To the printmakers, Lincoln's reelection meant little—at least temporarily. Only a handful of new print portraiture was published during the last five months of the President's life. If there was any new public interest in pictures of Lincoln, it was being satisfied by existing images.

One important exception came when, late in the war, one print artist, determined to create a faithful presidential likeness, enlisted Lincoln's personal help to achieve it. Elijah C. Middleton (1818–1883) had prepared a proof copy (Fig. 67) of a proposed chromolithograph which an intermediary brought to the President's attention. On December 30, 1864, Lincoln sent him this critique (see Fig. 69), written in a matter-of-fact tone indicating a new ease with such discussions:

> Your picture presented is, in the main, very good. From a line across immediately above the eyebrows, downward it appears to me perfect—Above such line I think it is not so good,—that is, while it gives perhaps a better fore-head, it is not quite true to the original. If you were present, I could tell you wherein, but I can not well do so on paper. The next best thing, I suppose, would be to carefully study a photograph.[56]

FIGURE 67. Middleton, Strobridge & Co., *Yours truly/A. Lincoln* (facsimile signature), Cincinnati, Ohio (*c.* 1864). Lithograph, 12 ¾ × 16 in. This crude print may have been the pose lithographer Middleton sent to Lincoln for his approval in 1864. If it is, Lincoln's mild criticism (see Fig. 69) is understandable. (*Louis A. Warren Lincoln Library and Museum*)

FIGURE 68. E[lijah]. C[hapman]
Middleton [*Abraham Lincoln*],
Cincinnati, Ohio (1864).
Chromolithograph in "warranted oil
colors," oval, 15 × 15 ¾ in. This is
the only print portrait of himself for
which Lincoln provided direct advice
to an artist. Lithographer Middleton
advertised himself as a producer of
"National Chromo Portraits and
Domestic Chromos." (*Louis A. Warren
Lincoln Library and Museum*)

It seems likely that Lincoln's suggestions were incorporated
into the final version of Middleton's chromo portrait (Fig. 68),
which was published by Middleton together with Hines Strobridge and Dominique C. Fabronious of Cincinnati. The surviving copies bear a striking resemblance to one of the photographs
Francis B. Carpenter had commissioned at Brady's on February 9,
1864 (Fig. 70), a pose which many printmakers would also adapt,
with inferior results, after Lincoln's death.

The artist had special reason for gratitude to Lincoln. The
previous September, Middleton had pleaded the case of his teen-
aged son, who had been taken prisoner by the Confederates.
Lincoln agreed to a special exchange if the father would furnish a
substitute soldier for his boy once he was released. The artist

FIGURE 69. Lincoln's letter to printmaker Elijah C. Middleton. *(New York Public Library)*

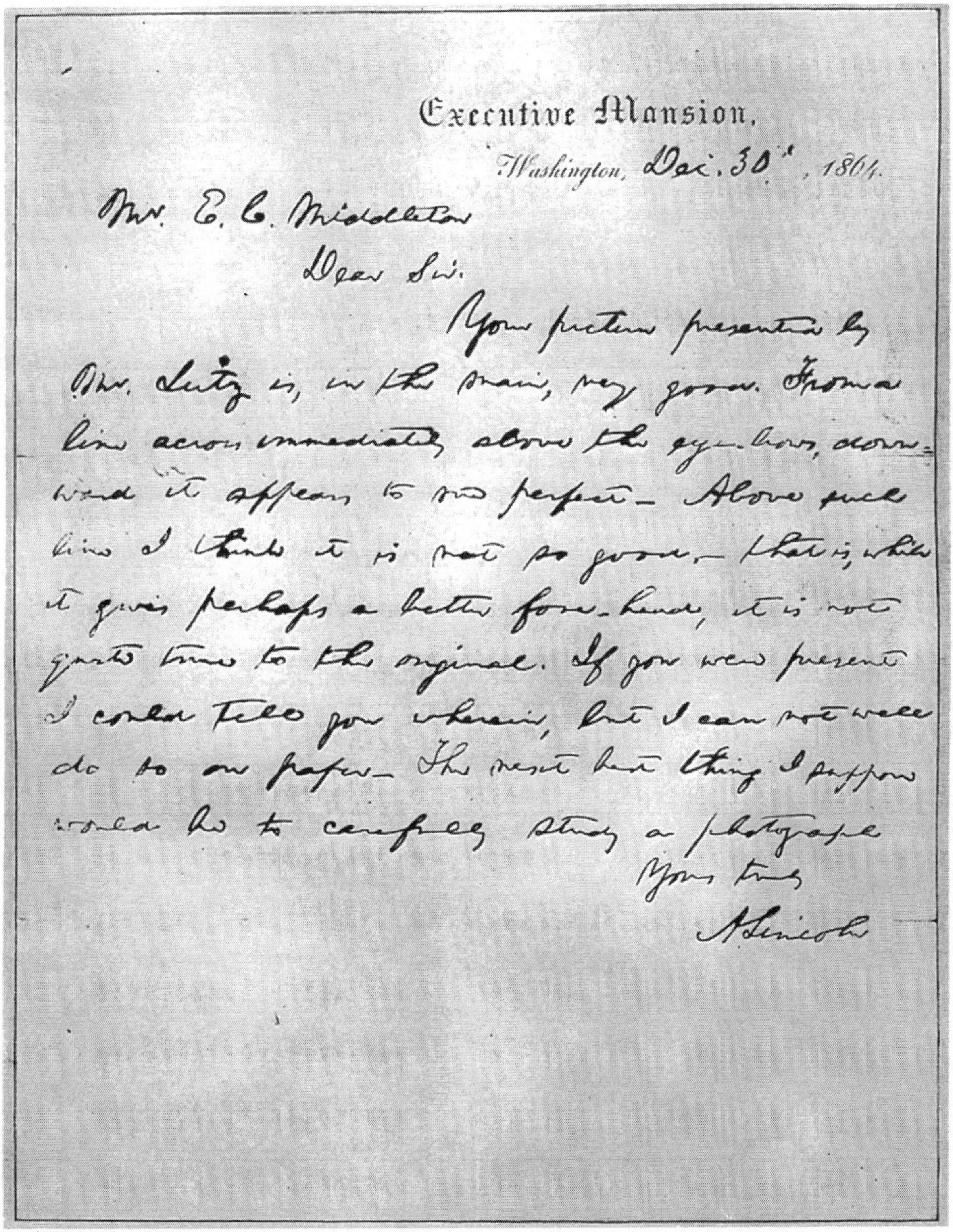

Executive Mansion,

Washington, Dec. 30th, 1864.

Mr. E. C. Middleton

Dear Sir:

Your picture presented by Mr. Lutz is, in the main, very good. From a line across immediately above the eye-brows, downward it appears to me perfect— Above such line I think it is not so good,— that is, while it gives perhaps a better fore-head, it is not quite true to the original. If you were present I could tell you wherein, but I can not well do so on paper— The next best thing I suppose would be to carefully study a photograph.

Yours truly

A. Lincoln

could later be grateful, too, for the popularity of Lincoln's portrait and those of other Civil War heroes done by Middleton's special method of printing on paper backed by canvas to look like a painting. It made the Ohio graphics entrepreneur a rich man.[57]

Between the appearance of Middleton's print and the assassination, few new Lincoln print portraits appeared. The last life painting of Lincoln (Fig. 71), completed in February 1865, inspired what was probably the last of his print portraits conceived during his lifetime, even though it was not published until after his death. In a sense, then, Matthew Wilson's (1814–1892) canvas and the lithographed adaptation by Louis Prang bridged two eras, one closely following, even overlapping, the other, in which Lincoln was portrayed first as Emancipator and then as Martyr.

Wilson's painting depicted a Lincoln much like the one the Canadian ornithologist-turned-intelligence agent A. M. Ross saw when he wrote:

> He looked much older, and bore traces of having passed through months of painful anxiety and trouble. There was a sad, serious look in his eyes that spoke louder than words of the disappointments, trials, and discouragements he had encountered since the war began. The wrinkles about the eyes and forehead were deeper: the lips were firmer, but indicative of kindness and forbearance. The great struggle had brought out the hidden riches of his noble nature.[58]

FIGURE 70. Photograph by the Brady studio, Washington, D.C. (February 9, 1864). This is the photograph consulted by Middleton in preparing his chromolithograph of Lincoln. (*Louis A. Warren Lincoln Library and Museum*)

And yet the faint glimmer of a smile was also discernible in Wilson's Lincoln, owing its expression to an Alexander Gardner photograph on which it was partly based. Near the end, the finished canvas hung on a wall in Lincoln's office. Gideon Welles,

FIGURE 71. Portrait from life by Matthew Wilson, Washington, D.C. (February, 1865). Oil on board, oval: 16 ⅞ × 13 ⅞ in. (*Louis A. Warren Lincoln Library and Museum*)

for whom it was painted, told Lincoln he thought it "a successful likeness," which prompted this reply from the President, as recorded by Carpenter: " 'Yes,' returned the President, hesitatingly; and then came a story of a western friend whose wife pronounced her husband's portrait, painted secretly for a birthday present, 'horridly like,' 'and that,' said he, 'seems to me a just criticism of this!' "[59]

Not unexpectedly, what had seemed so horridly like himself to the living Lincoln appeared the almost beatific visage of a newly anointed saint after the assassination. In retrospect, the portrait seemed to suggest grief melting away from this Lincoln, to reveal

FIGURE 72. Louis Prang, *Abraham Lincoln./Copied by permission from the original picture by Matthew Wilson—/ now in possession of Hon. Gideon Welles, Secy. of the Navy*, Boston (1865). Lithograph, 14 ⅞ × 18 in. According to Wilson's diaries, he painted one copy of his life portrait especially for use by the lithographer Louis Prang. Wilson completed it no earlier than May 1865, and this elegant print adaptation appeared shortly thereafter, probably one of the earliest post-assassination prints of Lincoln. *(Louis A. Warren Lincoln Library and Museum)*

ABRAHAM LINCOLN.

GRAND RECEPTION OF THE NOTABILITIES OF THE NATION

what Nicolay perceived in the Clark Mills life mask made the same month—"a peace that passeth understanding." Here was Lincoln reduced to the bare essentials of his humanity: stripped of girth, sapped of strength, but free at last from anguish—if only for the brief peace he would survive to enjoy.

Perhaps the painting and its print adaptation (Fig. 72) may not have revealed quite so much. But it may be reasonable to assume that contemporary audiences sought these reaffirmations as they studied such images. Lincoln had been Moses; now he was like Christ himself, dead for the sins of warring American brothers. He had become an icon.

Only a few days before Lincoln's death, Frank Leslie had published a lithograph (Fig. 73) of a "grand reception" at the White House, unaware it was to be the President's last such levee. The picture froze in time the Lincoln who might have emerged

FIGURE 73. [Henry B.] Major & [Joseph] Knapp, *Grand Reception of the Notabilities of the Nation,/At the White House 1865./Dedicated to Mrs. Abraham Lincoln/by the Publishers of Frank Leslie's Chimney Corner,* published by Frank Leslie, New York (1865). Lithograph, 20 3/8 × 15 in. Copyrighted on April 8, 1865, only a week before Lincoln's death, this may have been the last print portrait of the sixteenth President published during his lifetime. After Lincoln's death, a rival printmaker pirated the design, made a few alterations, and issued the result under the new title *Lincoln's Last Reception.* The originals had retailed for $3 each but were really published as a free premium for buyers of the first two issues of *The Chimney Corner,* a "new family paper." To make sure the paper's new readers remained loyal, Leslie promised to publish a "Key to this Plate," identifying the more than forty celebrities portrayed—but not until issue number four. *(Louis A. Warren Lincoln Library and Museum).* The key to *Grand Reception,* from the subsequent issue of the newspaper, did not appear until the month after Lincoln's death.

1. Senator Anthony. 2. Senator Fessenden. 3. Major-Gen. Foster. 4. Major-Gen. Sherman. 5. Hon. E. G. Squier. 6. Mrs. Stephens. 7. Senator Sumner. 8. Major-Gen. Kilpatrick. 9. Major-Gen. Banks. 10. Mrs. E. G. Squier. 11. Major-Gen. Sheridan. 12. Major-Gen. Hancock. 13. Admiral Farragut. 14. Governor Curtin. 15. Major-Gen. Logan. 16. Major-Gen. Hooker. 17. Hon. Horace Greeley. 18. Lieut.-Gen. Grant. 19. Major-Gen. Butler. 20. Hon. H. J. Raymond. 21. Admiral Porter. 22. Mrs. Gen. Grant. 23. President Johnson. 24. Major-Gen. Howard. 25. The late President Lincoln. 26. Major-Gen. Dix. 27. Mrs. Lincoln. 28. Chief Justice Chase. 29. Secretary Stanton. 30. Hon. Cassius C. Clay. 31. Mrs. Senator Sprague. 32. Major-Gen. Slocum. 33. Secretary Seward. 34. Speaker Colfax. 35. Mrs. Douglas. 36. Secretary Welles. 37. Mr. J. G. Bennett.

from his years of unrelieved melancholy—the catharsis denied him by John Wilkes Booth. Presiding at a cotillion graced by recognizable American celebrities, this was the slightly awkward but altogether winning Lincoln whom Walt Whitman saw "drest all in black, with white gloves and a claw-hammer coat, receiving, as if in duty bound, shaking hands, looking very disconsolate, as if he would give anything to be somewhere else."

At 7:30 A.M. on Saturday, April 15, church bells throughout the capital began tolling to announce that Abraham Lincoln was dead, and Whitman wrote in his notebook: "Black clouds driving overhead, Lincoln's death—black, black, black—as you look toward the sky—long broad black like great serpents."[60]

PART III

Apotheosis and Apocrypha

Yes, he had lived to shame me from my sneer,
To lame my pencil, and confute my pen—
To make me own this hind of princes peer,
This rail-splitter a true-born king of men.

—Tom Taylor in
Punch, May 6, 1865[1]

BEFORE HIS assassination on Good Friday, April 14, 1865, Abraham Lincoln had been many things to Americans: to some, politician, President, commander-in-chief, Emancipator; to others, tyrant, usurper, dictator, buffoon. After his death he became, above all else, in the words of historian Roy Basler, "the prophet, savior, and martyr." His assassin, John Wilkes Booth, in seeking revenge for the defeated South and an end to Lincoln's hold on the American people, accomplished precisely the reverse. As Basler said: "He gave the world a martyr and saint where it had once had a man."[2]

A contemporary of Lincoln's noted: "His greatness, his honesty . . . rise up to-day, and . . . transfigure him whom we called the 'common rail-splitter.' "[3] The railsplitter, Honest Abe, Lincoln the storyteller, Abe the flatboatman, even the tyrant and jokester—all these images were subordinated to the newer, more appropriate one exemplified in the title of one period lithograph: *The Martyr of Liberty* (Fig. 76). This redefinition of Lincoln's place in American thought, his swift transcendence from history into folklore, was one of the more remarkable cultural phenomena of our history. It was the product of many influences, including religious fervor, superstition, the retrospective impact of Lincoln's own last public utterances, and popular art. Lincoln the man was swallowed by the myth, a myth neither the passage of time nor the challenge of revisionist historians has been able to tarnish.

Lincoln himself set the stage for this transformation when, near the moment of conquest by the Union Army, he proposed a victory with compassion rather than vengeance. In retrospect, his recommendations would seem almost saintly. Lincoln himself thought that his Second Inaugural Address would "wear as well"

FIGURE 74. Kimmel & Forster, *The Last Offer of Reconciliation,/In Remembrance of Prest. A. Lincoln/"The Door Is Open to All,"* published by Henry & Wm. Vought, New York (1865). Lithograph, 24 ½ × 16 ⅞ in. One of the final entries in Kimmel & Forster's lithographic series on the history of the war (see Fig. 41), this print depicts within its charming vine borders surprisingly sympathetic portraits of Robert E. Lee and Jefferson Davis. The message of the print, forgiveness and restoration, contrasts sharply with the prevailing public mood in the wake of Lincoln's assassination, which was one of bitterness and vengeance. *(Louis A. Warren Lincoln Library and Museum)*

THE ASSASSINATION OF PRESIDENT LINCOLN
At Ford's Theatre, Washington, on the night of Friday, April 14, 1865.

as anything else he wrote, and his assassination ensured his prophecy:

> With malice toward none; with charity for all, with firmness in the right, as God gives us to see the right, let us strive on to finish the work we are in; to bind up the nation's wounds; to care for him who shall have borne the battle, and for his widow, and his orphan—to do all which may achieve and cherish a just, and a lasting peace, among ourselves, and with all nations.[4]

Four weeks after these words were spoken, Robert E. Lee surrendered his Army of Northern Virginia, ushering in a peace that brought Lincoln a "gladness of heart,"[5] a rejoicing that was echoed throughout the North. The leading cities rocked with celebration. For a week the public mood was jubilant. Then suddenly Lincoln was dead.

It was not lost on Americans that the tragedy had occurred on

FIGURE 75. [Printmaker unknown], *The Assassination of President Lincoln/At Ford's Theatre, Washington, on the night of Friday, April 14, 1865, (c. 1865).* Lithograph, 11 ¾ × 7 ¾ in. One of many Civil War prints that attests to the lack of visual sophistication in midnineteenth-century America, this assassination scene, with its grossly distorted perspective, offers a strange mixture of careful detail and wild inaccuracy. The spur that caused Booth to break his leg lies on the stage, for example, but the flag in which he snagged it is not draped over the President's box, itself shown much too near stage level. In addition, Lincoln slumped over in his chair after the shot and did not stand, as this lithograph suggests. *(Louis A. Warren Lincoln Library and Museum)*

THE MARTYR OF LIBERTY.

Hath borne his faculties so meek; has been
So clear in his great office; that his virtues
Shall plead, trumped-tongued, against
The deep damnation of his taking off."

Good Friday, nor that Lincoln had proclaimed in his Inaugural Address: "The Almighty has His own purposes . . . the judgments of the Lord, are true and righteous altogether." Now those words were reinterpreted as a foreboding of immortality, made almost divine by the fact that the murder had taken place on a holy day (on which, ironically enough, the living Lincoln had chosen not to pray but to attend the theater—a transgression seldom mentioned after his assassination). "Heaven," Ralph Waldo Emerson noted, "wishing to show the world a completed benefactor, shall make him serve his country even more by his death than by his life."[6]

Easter Sunday was traditionally the festival of flowers. But Easter Sunday 1865 became "Black Easter" in the North. Mourning crêpe replaced white floral arrangements as the dominant motif in American churches, and from pulpits across the country, clergymen introduced the mystical connections that linked Lincoln's death to the original Good Friday martyrdom in Judea. All

FIGURE 76. [Printmaker unknown], *The Martyr of Liberty* (c. 1865). Lithograph, 8¼ × 9⅞ in. Another example of the myriad assassination scenes that flooded the country after Lincoln's death, this otherwise mundane print is elevated by the inclusion of a profound and literate allusion from Shakespeare. The print features an adaptation of Macbeth's famous "vaulting ambition" soliloquy, with only the introduction changed, from "This Duncan" to "This Lincoln." The reworked speech may be interpreted, in one sense, as coming from Booth as he shoots the President and therefore almost as a justification for murder. Macbeth said the lines as he contemplated assassinating King Duncan. In broader terms, the poetry represents the national feeling at Lincoln's death and apotheosis. The unknown printmaker's use of the verse is particualrly intriguing because *Macbeth* was Lincoln's favorite Shakespearean play. Interestingly, he was fascinated by another of Macbeth's ruminations, this one on political assassination—the "Duncan is in his grave" speech, which Macbeth recites after killing the king: "After life's fitful fever he sleeps well;/Treason has done his worst: nor steel, nor poison,/Malice domestic, foreign levy, nothing/Can touch him further" (Lincoln recited it for Senator Sumner; see Isaac N. Arnold, *The Life of Abraham Lincoln*, Chicago: McClurg, 1906, p. 444.) *(Louis A. Warren Lincoln Library and Museum)*

THE LAST MOMENTS OF ABRAHAM LINCOLN ⚔ PRESIDENT OF THE UNITED STATES.

FIGURE 77. Max Rosenthal, *The Last Moments of Abraham Lincoln/President of the United States*, "engraved" by Rosenthal after a design by Joseph Hoover, printed by L. N. Rosenthal, and published by Hoover; copyrighted by George T. Perry, Philadelphia (1865). Hand-colored lithograph, 23 × 17 ⅞ in. The artist gave several of the portraits a pudgy, spherical look untrue to the originals. (*Library of Congress*)

seemed to agree that once again God had moved in mysterious ways.

So rapid was Lincoln's apotheosis that some pastors preached that God had ordained Lincoln's death because America had begun revering its President "impiously." Said a Troy, New York, minister: "God is a jealous God and will not suffer the honor and glory that are due himself to be ascribed to any creature. God will punish idolatry." Added a New York preacher: "No man is great enough, nor good enough to share the honors of the House of God." Such warnings only made Lincoln seem the greater.[7]

Other pastors suggested that Lincoln had been taken because of the conciliatory policy he had urged in dealing with the South. Perhaps he had been too good a man also to have been a just

FIGURE 79. J. L. Magee, *Satan Tempting Booth to the Murder of the President*, Philadelphia (1865). Lithograph, 5 ¾ × 8 in. Though the symbolism of this print is crude, the artistic conception is superior, and it is vastly better in execution than Magee's deathbed scene (Fig. 78). By the uncertain manner in which he grasps his weapon and the thoughtful expression in his eyes, Booth appears genuinely to be contemplating the crime he is about to commit. There is even dramatic tension to the scene: in the background we see Lincoln enjoying the play at Ford's Theatre. Although we know he will be assassinated, we are led visually to believe, by viewing the living man, that at this moment of unholy influence there is still a chance the President might escape his fate. *(Louis A. Warren Lincoln Library and Museum)*

man. "There are those . . . who think that Providence has permitted this calamity to befall us that a sterner hand might rule in our national affairs," suggested a Methodist minister in New York. "May it not be," inquired a Brooklyn minister, "that God has permitted this great crime to awaken us to a sense of justice and to a full exactation of God's law upon those who have planned and accomplished the horrible scenes of the past four years?" A Connecticut preacher saw "a divine interest to dry up all fountains of false sympathy and to bring the land to a proper sense of duty." And to a Cincinnati pastor, Lincoln fell at the height of his glory "in order that mercy should not become a crime." It was as if Lincoln's death permitted both mourning for the man of mercy and a concurrent release of the passion for revenge which Lincoln, as President, had tried to hold in check. Lincoln could then become a figure to be worshipped, precisely so that his example would not always have to be followed.[8]

Booth was damned as a "second Judas," whose crime was "not only assassination" but "parricide; for Abraham Lincoln was as a father to the whole nation." God had left George Washington "childless so that, by a grateful people, he would always be called by the name of Father of the Nation! And now another father of his country has been taken from us, thus rudely the crown of martyrdom is his." He was also likened to Moses, who "had passed through battle, sorrow and war; had climbed the heights," and then died once the Lord "showed him all the land." Or he was Christ reincarnate, perishing in a modern "week of sorrows, in gloom and blood." Many pastors noted that "Good Friday was the day, of all days in the year, chosen by the murderer for his infamous deed[.] It is one of those remarkable historical coincidences" which would convince the faithful that "could our Presi-

FIGURE 78. J[ohn]. L. Magee, *Death Bed of Abraham Lincoln./Died April 15th, 1865*, Philadelphia (1865). Lithograph, 14 × 9 ¼ in. One of the oddest of the deathbed prints of Lincoln, this lithograph features a host of bizarre elements: a dwarflike Secretary of War Stanton (far left), the administration of the last rites of the Catholic Church—not Lincoln's religion (foreground)—and the victim holding hands with Vice-President Andrew Johnson. In the background, center, Mrs. Lincoln, depicted swooning in the arms of her son, might seem to the irreverent viewer to be stealing an incestuous kiss. *(Louis A. Warren Lincoln Library and Museum)*

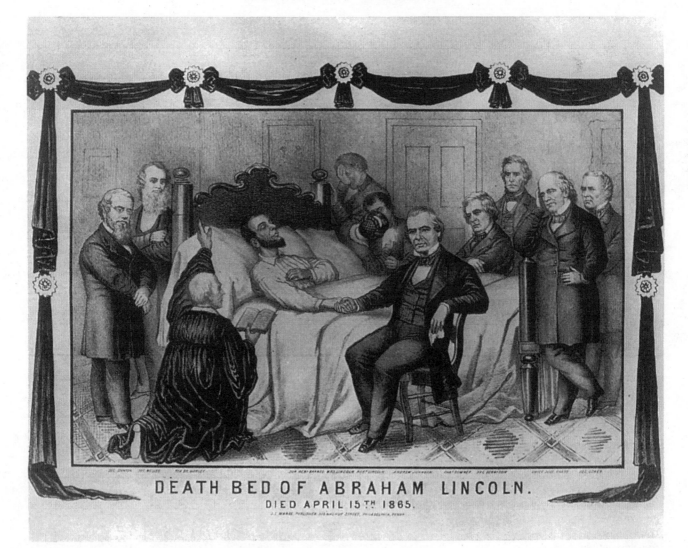

DEATH BED OF ABRAHAM LINCOLN.
DIED APRIL 15TH 1865.

SATAN TEMPTING BOOTH TO THE MURDER OF THE PRESIDENT.

J.L. MAGEE, PUB. 305 WALNUT ST. PHILAD^a

dent have spoken after he was shot, he would have forgiven the cowardly perpetrator of this inhuman act, and rounded the parallel with a final and complete imitation of our Lord's example." The pastor of St. Paul's Church in New York City summed it up this way: "His death was on Good Friday, and his last official words were, in substance, 'Father, forgive them for they know not what they do.' "[9]

Lincoln's critics were silenced. *Punch,* the British humor magazine that had consistently attacked Lincoln in cartoons as well as editorials, now did an about-face, publishing a famous poetic retraction by editor Tom Taylor (see the opening of this chapter). Taylor ordered the artist John Tenniel to draw a sentimental obituary cartoon, *Britannia Sympathizes with Columbia,* in which the female symbol of England laid a wreath on Lincoln's draped corpse while another female figure and a freedman crouched weeping in the foreground. One member of the magazine's staff remarked that Taylor "had not only made *P[unch]* eat humble pie, but swallow dish and all."[10]

The visual metamorphosis was beginning. Lincoln's remains were taken back to the White House, where he lay in state, thousands lining up to gaze "once more upon the features of him who had in life so won the affections of the people." These same features only a few months before had been mocked by his enemies and discussed with embarrassment even by his supporters. Now, he had been transfigured, "more sincerely lamented than any public man of these times or of this nation." In the span of a few weeks, "More people . . . gazed on the face of the departed than have ever looked upon the face of any other departed man." Most suddenly found it beautiful, "as if in a quiet sleep." True to the folk myth of the dying god, the historian

Lloyd Lewis wrote, even this homely martyr was now to be remembered as "beautiful of face and soul, kind and gentle," like others of the breed who, in folklore, poured out "their blood with patient gladness that Man may live and prosper."[11]

Observed one of Lincoln's contemporaries: "Yesterday, his detractors were ridiculing his large hands without gloves, his large feet . . . to-day this type which we found grotesque appears to us on the threshhold of immortality, and we understand by the universality of our grief what future generations will see in him." Now, wrote the poet Eugene J. Hall,

> O furrowed face, beloved by all the nation!
>   O tall gaunt form, to memory fondly dear. . . .
> You fell! An anxious nation's hopes seemed blighted,
>   While millions shuddered at your dreadful fall. . . .[12]

Poets composed odes to the martyr. Journalists wired detailed reports of the continuing national mourning while Lincoln's body traveled for funerals in New York, Philadelphia, Chicago, and other cities. As the days passed, printmakers, too, seized the opportunity to catch up with the writers, to join in the effort to shape and exploit the outpouring of grief.

Evidence of the developing need to recreate the lost Lincoln in pictures could be found in New York as soon as the President's body arrived there for the spectacular funeral. The city was a Democratic stronghold and had never supported Lincoln; it had been the scene of secession threats in 1861 and draft riots in 1863. In 1865, however, partisanship was forgotten, and New York lay "crushed into universal sorrow and lamentation by the brutal assassination."[13]

FIGURE 80. William Sartain after a painting by S[amuel]. B[ell]. Waugh (1814–1885), *Lincoln and His Family*, published by Bradley & Co., Philadelphia, and by H. Curran, Rochester, N.Y. (1866). Mezzotint engraving, 24 ¾ × 17 ¾ in. Sartain's was an expensive print: $20 for artist's proofs, $14 for india proofs, $10 for plain proofs, and $7.25 for "plain prints." This print proved so popular it was soon adapted by period photographers and republished as *cartes-de-visite*, resulting in the illusion that they were genuine photographs of the Lincoln family. (*Mr. and Mrs. G. S. Boritt*)

The houses, shops, and office buildings of the great metropolis were quickly decorated with signs of mourning and respect. A contemporary witness claimed that "scarcely a building in the city, public or private, from the palatial Fifth Avenue mansion to the humblest tenement house, could be seen, which had not some outward funereal decoration; while nearly all our citizens wore mourning badges upon their persons." Before long, the available stockpile of mourning goods was "nearly exhausted." From Battery Park to Union Square, New York was cloaked in "a garb of sorrow."[14]

Drapery, flags, ribbons, and crêpe were festooned around pillars, poles, and streetlights, and in shop and parlor windows. Lincoln portraiture was in evidence as well, in offices, stores, homes, houses of worship, and even police precincts. The custom house displayed busts of Washington, Jackson, Clay, Scott, and Webster, all draped, alongside a bust of the "martyred President," kept bare of any drapery or "sorrow-suggesting emblems."

"The thoughts occasioned by the mere view of that face are sufficiently saddening," a witness explained, "without the assistance of any mournful symbols."[15]

Clarke's Photographic Union displayed a "well-painted transparency of the President, and underneath, the words: 'His memory, like the Union he preserved, is not for a day, but for all time." A major Broadway emporium displayed a large Lincoln portrait captioned: "We shall not look upon his like again." Fox's old Bowery Theatre hung "a large portrait of the President, beneath which was the motto: 'We mourn the loss of an honest man. ' " At Loder & Co., "a finely executed engraving of the late President, placed in one of the lower windows, appropriately draped, attracted general attention." And the Bowery Savings Bank displayed "a portrait . . . and over it the words: 'Our country weeps. In God we trust. ' "[16]

The display of likenesses seemed universal. "Many private houses," reported one newspaper, "had portraits of the late Mr. Lincoln suspended from the upper windows, surrounded with crape, &c," as "flags, looped with crape, hung across the streets, and drooped from tops of churches and many public buildings." People "seemed to regard the death of Abraham Lincoln as if death had carried off one of their own members . . ." as in ancient Egypt after the plagues, where "there was not a house in which there was not one dead."[17]

Churches discarded Easter decorations to make way for "emblems of death," and parishioners took to wearing mourning ribbons "containing a small picture of the deceased." A "fine portrait" won approval at a local police station, while "the portraits of the late President . . . exhibited in the print-shops, were gazed at by large crowds."[18]

In the weeks to come, the printshops would do far more than display single images in the windows. Once the immediate day of mourning passed and the stores and businesses reopened, print-makers would begin churning out an overwhelming quantity of Lincoln pictures: assassination and deathbed scenes to respond to the need for visualizations of the awful deed and its aftermath; sheet music covers to decorate funeral compositions; reverential portraiture that celebrated the martyr in romantic picture and caption, disguising all flaws in an attempt to heroize and mythify; new Emancipation tributes to the modern Moses; fanciful pictures of Lincoln with George Washington; scenes portraying the Lincoln family at home; and scenes from his early life, their importance now exaggerated to make them equal to the man who had become a martyr.

It did take the print industry a little while to respond, as contemporary advertisements for mourning pictures show. The first issue of *Harper's Weekly* to contain assassination news and illustrations was dated April 22, 1865. The April 29 issue was the first to contain advertisements for any products related to the assassination—in this case, photographs of John Wilkes Booth. It was not until May 6 that advertisements for medals, mourning badges, and photographs of Lincoln appeared. The May 6 issue of *Harper's Weekly* was an important one for the print industry, and for Lincoln's image thereafter, because it published on the cover a woodcut based on a charming photograph of Lincoln with his son Tad (see Fig. 82). Copies of the photograph, which had been taken over a year earlier, had almost certainly been available at Brady's studios before the assassination, but it required the sharp eye of an illustrated newspaper to realize that this photograph

LINCOLN FAMILY

offered great possibilities, especially as a mourning emblem for the murdered President.

Amid the ballyhooed cures for piles, stammering, and cancer appeared on May 13 the first advertisements for new Lincoln prints: funeral sheet music, a "just completed" steel engraving (as well as John Sartain's old ones), and—remarkably—*President Lincoln Reading the Bible to His Son Tad.* The last named was a lithographed version of the Lincoln and Tad pose; only now the photograph album in the President's lap was described as a Bible.

Funeral music, 40 cents with portrait and 30 cents plain, continued to be advertised until July 1. Hawkers of mourning pins declared, "Mourning to last for 60 days," but "splendid mourning pictures" and "Lincoln at Home" prints appeared in advertisements more than sixty days after April 15. By July 15, however, all ads for Lincoln pictures had disappeared, and only one for a biography of Lincoln remained as a reminder of the

FIGURE 81. Charles Hart, *Lincoln Family,* New York (1866). Lithograph, 24 × 17 ¼ in. A sales circular for the Sartain family print (Fig. 80) had declared: "The law of copyright and the Publisher's agreements with the Artists, prevent others from engraving from them, so that all who wish copies . . . must procure them from our salesmen. . . . From no other sources can these . . . be procured, now or in the future." Hart found one way around this supposedly ironclad copyright guarantee; for the print above, he pirated the Sartain and issued it as a thinly disguised mirror image. His portraits are considerably cruder than the gifted Sartain's. *(Louis A. Warren Lincoln Library and Museum)*

assassination. On July 22 there were no advertisements for any sort of Lincoln item in *Harper's* columns, even though this was the issue which carried the first woodcuts showing the hanging of John Wilkes Booth's co-conspirators. A poem by Charles Halpine commemorating the Battle of Gettysburg published in the newspaper contained no mention of or literary allusion to Lincoln's Gettysburg Address.[19]

The phenomenon was over. It had taken the industry about three or four weeks to respond, and the surge in demand lasted less than two months after that. Many Lincoln items published shortly after his death were undated, but the safest guess is that the bulk of them also appeared between May 15 and July 15, 1865. Nevertheless, the immediate artistic response left its mark on Lincoln's image ever after.

The death of George Washington in 1799 had inspired similar "patriotic grief and commercial zeal." If print art was indeed heir to the religious picture, then Lincoln was its most obvious, most appealing subject: an American icon deified in the classical tradition of the dying god, martyred symbolically, on the anniversary of history's most famous martyrdom, linked by deed to Washington, and by virtue and violent death to Jesus Christ himself.[20]

Prints were not the medium of subtlety. John Wilkes Booth would now be portrayed as the tool of the devil himself (see Fig. 79), while angels would be depicted accompanying Lincoln to heaven, to be greeted there by Washington—with whom, of course, he was never portrayed until his assassination (see Figs. 94–96). Statesmanship on a par with Washington's was truly within the ability only of dead politicians. It was one example of a body of work that represented in part a sentimental counterattack to the years of political caricature. Earlier prints had been designed only to introduce Lincoln or to make his deeds palatable to the electorate. Something much more ambitious would be attempted now: a visual transformation.

Currier & Ives's hand-colored lithograph of the assassination, fairly accurate in its presentation of the event and its placement of the principal characters, was but one of dozens of prints quickly issued to meet the initial public demand. These were scenes of the shooting itself. Such prints offered wildly differing perspectives on the murder. Booth was portrayed variously as a Satanically inspired instrument of evil or a rather romantic-looking actor playing an unsympathetic role. Lincoln was made to appear instantly comatose or suffering great pain or, in one marvelous product of an anonymous lithographer's imagination, able to rise to his feet as if preparing to deliver an oration (see Fig. 75). Although all these scenes were created to satisfy the national curiosity over details of the tragedy, none of the efforts was entirely accurate, and none captured the violence, horror, or awesome historical importance of the event.

Like the deathbed scenes produced as companion prints to the assassination portrayals, these pictures were as cosmeticized as the Lincoln corpse that had toured the country on the journey to its Springfield grave. The morticians had repaired Lincoln's wound and petrified him for the long series of funerals, guaranteeing that mourners would be spared the grisly sight of the aftereffects of death by gunfire. When Lincoln's old friend Orville Hickman Browning first inspected the embalmed body, he found it "greatly changed" since Lincoln's death, "the eyes . . . returned to their sockets and all discoloration gone."[21] Similarly, the printmakers sanitized their Lincoln murder and deathbed scenes, offering sentimentalized and subdued depictions, nearly all showing the victim at peace, sleeping his way to heaven (see Fig. 77). Blood was rarely shown. Since such pictures provided the sole mirror through which Americans could witness the tragedy, few were ever able to understand the medical realities of Lincoln's wound, his death struggle, or its effect on those with him when he was shot.

In deathbed scenes, Lincoln was shown without pain or discomfort, lacking the black pallor that Orville Browning noticed had discolored his face by the morning of his death. His surgeons were depicted sitting stoically at his side and not at work furiously, as they actually had been, laboring to keep Lincoln's wound open and free from clots so he could breathe, periodically cleaning the blood and brain tissue from his pillows, struggling to keep his body temperature up.

The group of important people who attended Lincoln at his deathbed was also routinely exaggerated and falsified in print portraits of the day. Lincoln died in a tiny bedchamber capable of holding no more than six or seven people at a time, but most prints portrayed at least a dozen at the vigil. One engraving, by A. H. Ritchie, showed twenty-six people in the room, and a painting issued years later as a gravure print depicted forty-six! Apparently, many picture publishers thought the public would not accept the grim reality of the scene of Lincoln's death: a claustrophobic, commonly furnished back bedroom in an ordinary Washington rooming house.[22]

Nor was the true cast of witnesses faithfully investigated or reported in these engravings and lithographs. More often than not, printmakers selected for inclusion in these scenes the most appropriate set of attendants, regardless of whether or not they had actually been in the death room. Occasionally, for example, such prints depicted Lincoln's youngest son, Tad, at the scene, although in reality he had not been allowed to leave the White House once news reached the mansion that his father had been shot. Chief Justice Salmon P. Chase was depicted in several prints of the death of Lincoln, although he was the one major government official who failed to make even a perfunctory visit to the scene. And Vice-President Andrew Johnson was almost always portrayed—the earliest Currier & Ives lithograph had omitted him, but subsequent revisions placed him where General Henry Halleck had stood in the original—even though his visit to the deathbed had been brief, and he had not remained to witness Lincoln's actual death, as the prints implied.

Finally, there was the problem of what to do with Mary herself. Secretary of War Edwin M. Stanton, who had taken charge in the Petersen House that night, had barred Mrs. Lincoln from the death room altogether, once her outbursts grew unbearable to the other attendants. She was not present at her husband's bedside when he died at 7:22 the morning after the shooting. Hence, all the prints that portrayed her calmly sitting by Lincoln's bedside technically erred. But it is doubtful whether factual pictorial reporting would have satisfied an American audience overcome with sympathy and sentiment, who wished this American family to be united in death.

For this reason, Lincoln's death soon inspired a body of post-assassination print portraits designed to reinforce his emerging status as folk hero. He would be portrayed not only as the central figure of his family circle, but in council with his generals (Fig. 65), en route to heaven with George Washington, even in a personal offer of reconciliation to Jefferson Davis (Fig. 74)—all scenes that seemed to touch a responsive chord once Lincoln's assassination had elevated him to a new plateau.

The richest body of work consisted of the countless different depictions of the Lincoln family, all of which seemed to have in common the aim of showing Lincoln at a happier time in his life. Ironically, none of the family prints was issued until after his death, when the public was given its first look past the closed doors of the White House and into parlor scenes that had more to do with the printmakers' imagination than the realities of Lincoln's home life.

The Lincoln family prints played a large role in shaping the Lincoln image. If a President had no home, he was an entirely public man—all calculation, all ambition, all business—and he would lack "sympathy, honor, or virtue."[23] He would have no refuge from the cares of office.

In truth, during his term in office Lincoln had very little refuge. He could not get from his office in the Executive Mansion to his living quarters without passing through the very corridor in which people were queued up waiting to be admitted to his presence. It was not in Lincoln's nature to pass through such a throng without stopping to talk, and he arrived considerably later and tireder than when he started. Only in 1864 did he gain direct access to the family apartments by having a new door cut from his office.[24]

The President worked hard. Mrs. Lincoln complained in 1864 to an old girlhood friend: "I consider myself fortunate, if at eleven o'clock I once more find myself, in my pleasant room & very especially, if my tired & weary Husband, is *there*, resting in the lounge to receive me—to chat over the occurrences of the day."[25] The burdens of the presidency are not conducive to a rich family life, and the Lincolns experienced extraordinary external pressures and family tragedies responsible for a growing distance between Mr. and Mrs. Lincoln.

Mary maintained a rigorous mourning for almost three years after the death of their young son William Wallace (Willie) Lincoln on February 5, 1862. Her gloomy seclusion made family life so dark that Lincoln once warned her that excessive grief might force him to send her to "that large white building on the hill yonder," the Washington insane asylum.[26] Mary began trying to escape unpleasant associations by travel, at this period aimed at avoiding the sorrows, the summer heat, and the allegedly unhealthy climate of Washington. She also spent money compulsively, kept her debts secret from her husband, and worried that failure to gain reelection and four more years of presidential prestige and credit would cause him to discover her deception. She admitted that in their last carriage ride together, on the afternoon of the very day Lincoln was shot, he insisted that they "must *both*, be more cheerful in the future—between the war & the loss of our darling Willie—we have both, been very miserable."[27]

The Lincoln family was rarely together during the war years, although that is how the printmakers portrayed them. Among the purchasers of these prints, few realized how wildly imaginary they were: the family could no longer get together after 1860, in part because one son (Willie) died in 1862, in part because another (Robert) was almost grown, and, most important, because the presidency in wartime was wholly destructive of family life.

Willie's death early in 1862 limited to less than one year the time in which Mary and Abraham might have sat in their parlor

with Willie, Tad, and Robert. During that short period, Robert was a student at Harvard. He was in Washington for his father's inauguration but went back to Cambridge, "sick of Washington and glad to get back to his college," the next day. He was home for vacation in May, late July to early August, and Christmas 1861. He returned in February 1862 to be at his little brother's deathbed. After graduation from Harvard in 1864, Robert became an Army captain on General Ulysses S. Grant's staff. Those pictures which, like the one published by William Smith (Fig. 87), showed Robert in uniform with Willie, Tad, and their parents, were anachronistic. Those depicting Robert in mufti with both his brothers portrayed events that might have occurred only at three brief moments in 1861.[28]

William Sartain's mezzotint (see Fig. 80)—together with its *carte-de-visite*—was a scrupulously accurate depiction of the family as it might have appeared after Willie's death. Had Robert been at home in civilian clothes, his mother would likely have been in black mourning dress for Willie. In its day, the Sartain engraving was considered the best print portrait of the Lincoln family. A period circular for this "first class engraving" described the Samuel Waugh painting after which the print was modeled as "a great triumph of art." Boasted the circular: "For a number of months, Mr. Wm. Sartain, with an able corps of assistants, was actively engaged in copying and engraving from this superb painting. . . ." The result, its advertisers declared, "in accuracy of portraiture and artistic excellence of execution is acknowledged to be unsurpassed by any Engraving ever executed in America."

Point by point, character by character, the circular described the design of the print "from Waugh's Great Painting":

FIGURE 82. Photograph of Lincoln and his son Thomas (Tad) by the Brady studio, Washington, D.C. (February 9, 1864). (*Louis A. Warren Lincoln Library and Museum*)

The President and Mrs. Lincoln are seated at a table, back of which is Captain Robert Lincoln, standing in a manly and pleasing attitude. Little "Tad," the idol of his Father and the pet of the White House, sits upon an ottoman at his Father's side, leaning against him, and looking up with a happy, winning expression which draws all true hearts in sympathy toward him. Upon the wall, in the background, hangs a portrait of Willie, who died during Mr. Lincoln's first Presidential term.

On the table is a vase of flowers—embracing the Roses of the North, and the Small Magnolia, Sweet Clematis, and Virginia Creeper, which bloom in profusion in the South,—all wreathed in harmony, emblematical of the friendly feeling that *should* exist between the people of the North and South, in the great vase of the UNION. . . .

The grouping is graceful and harmonious. The President is in earnest conversation in regard to the future of our country. . . . The Artist has, with happy effect, thrown into his countenance that life and animation which he was accustomed to display in cheerful and animated conversation.

FIGURE 83. [Printmaker unknown], [*Lincoln and Tad*], published by John Smith, Philadelphia (*c.* 1865). Hand-colored lithograph, 18 ½ × 24 in. One of several prints based on the best "domestic" Lincoln photograph (Fig. 82), this lithograph showed a typical mix of skill (in drawing the chair) and crudeness (in the portraiture and anatomy), of slavish copying (the book in Lincoln's lap) and seemingly artful adaptation (the fringe on the chair and the chair's higher back). (*Louis A. Warren Lincoln Library and Museum*)

Excerpts from favorable press notices were also printed in the advertising circular. The Schenectady, New York, *Daily Evening Star* said: "Citizens will do well to secure" this gem "of art, before purchasing those cheap and inferior engravings with which the country is flooded." The Boston *Post* called the Sartain "one of the best artistic productions of its kind," predicting that it would "be almost universally sought for" and "a desirable picture for thousands of homes in the land." The Cleveland *Herald* termed it "among our first ranks of art," and the Troy *Daily Whig* praised it as a "new, large and exquisitely beautiful Steel Engraving of America's Great Matryr. . . ."

"Sartain Again Triumphant!" declared the Schenectady *Daily Union.* "It is not a common, cheap print, but really a superb work of art, and *the only satisfactory one on this subject now before the public.*" As the brochure declared. *"The figure of Lincoln alone is worth the price of the Engraving."*[29] A plain print was offered for $7.25, a plain proof for $10, an india proof for $15, and an artist's proof for $20—all steep prices in 1866. But a good print of the Lincoln family was by then overdue and the print became a best seller, to judge from the large number of copies that have survived. It did not seem to matter that the impulse for its creation was wrong: the Lincoln family was not coming together in the period depicted by Sartain; it was coming apart.

Victorian America's ideal of the sanctity of the family vanquished any such realities. The ideal was so powerful that President Lincoln himself had emphasized the sanctity of the Union and ridiculed secession by calling Southern constitutional doctrine a "sort of free-love arrangement."[30] Careful thinkers were sure that in the family lay the ultimate origins even of political loyalty. Horace Bushnell, a brilliant Connecticut Congregationalist minister and an ardent Republican, set out to write a book on the origins of national loyalty and political obligations and in the end wrote a book on the family. He called it *Christian Nurture,* and it appeared—significantly—in 1861.[31] Everyone knew that the family was important.

Lincoln knew it. Yet for all his apparent accommodation to the image-making process, he remained after four years in office strangely unaware of the full uses of any medium but the printed word. He never bothered to be photographed with his wife, and it was 1864 before he provided any photograph that could serve as a model for domestic images—the charming photograph with his

THE LINCOLN FAMILY

son Tad looking at a book in his father's lap, which *Harper's Weekly* made famous only after Lincoln's death.

Once again, Francis B. Carpenter was the genius behind one of the most lasting Lincoln images. It was Carpenter who composed the Lincoln and Tad photograph in Mathew Brady's Washington studio. (Anthony Berger shot the picture.) Ultimately, Carpenter frittered away the possible fruits of his genius by taking too long to finish the family painting he designed around it. He took the idea of a family portrait to engraver J. C. Buttre, who offered $500 for the right to adapt it into a print. Then Buttre rejected the painting Carpenter eventually showed him—in which, for the only time that anyone knows of, all the living Lincoln family members were painted from life. Buttre wanted Willie in the portrait, too. Carpenter finally worked up a chiaroscuro painting (for quick adaptation into a black-and-white print) of the family as it looked in 1861, and Buttre produced an engraving from it in 1867.[32]

To assemble models for the picture, Carpenter asked Mrs.

FIGURE 84. Haskell & Allen, *The Lincoln Family*, Boston (*c.* 1865). Lithograph, 12 ¾ × 8 ¼ in. In this expansion of the central grouping from the Brady photograph (Fig. 82), the printmakers added Robert and Mary and seated them in a family circle. The portrait of Mary appears to be based on an 1863 photograph, also taken by Brady's studio (Lloyd Ostendorf, *The Photographs of Mary Todd Lincoln,* Illinois State Historical Society, Springfield, 1969, p. 52.) (*Louis A. Warren Lincoln Library and Museum*)

FIGURE 85. *The Lincoln Family in 1861*, painting from photographs and life sketches by Francis Bicknell Carpenter (1865). Oil on canvas, 36 ¾ × 27 in. Carpenter explained this painting in 1895: "It was painted in black and white, with the expressed purpose of facilitating the engraving. When that was completed, I fully intended to finish the painting by adding color to the flesh as well as to the draperies. I never considered it finished any farther than as a model for the engraving" (Quoted in the *New York Historical Society Catalogue of American Portraits*, New Haven: Yale University Press, 1974, I, 465). *(New-York Historical Society)*

Lincoln to sit for a photograph. But the widow replied that "it would be utterly impossible for me, in my present nervous state, to sit." Mary did not like the photograph Carpenter then proposed as a model because "my hands are always *made* in *them*, very large and I look too stern. The drapery of the dress, was *not* sufficiently flowing—and my hair, should not be so low down, on the forehead & so much dressed." Instead, she urged the artist to consult "an excellent painted likeness of me, at Brady's in N.Y. taken in 1861. . . . I am sure you will like it & I believe, it was taken, in a black velvet." Mary did enclose a photograph "of my precious, sainted Willie."[33]

Mrs. Lincoln included instructions as to where to obtain "the best likeness" of Robert ("at Goldin's, in Washington, taken last Spring"), with the apology, "We have none, unframed." Finally there arrived from the widow another relic from the family album, a photograph of Willie and Tad together, taken in 1861, with the advice, "They will answer very well, for the picture, you propose painting." The mother cautioned, however: "Even, in *that* like-

FIGURE 86. J[ohn]. C[hester]. Buttre after a painting by Francis B. Carpenter, *The Lincoln Family,* New York (1867). Mezzotint engraving, 24 ¼ × 17 ¾ in. Writing of the plans to publish this print, Carpenter said: "Mr. Buttre proposes to engrave the picture in superb style—to be published only by subscription. I commend him to the kind consideration of my friends." (*Louis A. Warren Lincoln Library and Museum*)

LINCOLN AND HIS FAMILY.

FIGURE 87. D. Wiest after a drawing by A. Biegemann, *Lincoln and His Family*, published by William Smith, Philadelphia (*c.* 1865). Tinted lithograph, 24 ¼ × 18 ⅛ in. The perspective is so primitive in this print that the viewer might reasonably expect the books on top of the central table to slide at any moment onto the White House floor. The family members vary wildly in size and proportion, ranging from the gargantuan bloated eldest son, Robert, to a miniature child, meant to represent Tad, dressed almost as if he were an attendant at court. The middle child bears close resemblance to the real Tad, as one might expect, since his portrait is based on the Brady photograph of him (Fig. 82), but is meant to be Willie, who died in 1862. *(Louis A. Warren Lincoln Library and Museum)*

ness, of Willie, justice, is not done him, he was a very beautiful boy, with a most *spiritual* expression of face.... It is impossible, for *time*, to alleviate, the anguish of *such irreparable losses*—only the Grace of God, can calm our grief & still the tempest."[34]

Despite the intimacy of this "collaboration" between former First Lady and former White House artist-in-residence, it is not surprising that a modern scholar has observed of the family picture Carpenter later painted (Fig. 85), that he had done the portrait "in a servile manner from different photographs of the family," down to the background, whose "flatness recalls the backdrops commonly used by photographers."[35]

John Chester Buttre (1821–1893), who may have engraved three thousand plates during his long career as a printmaker, spent $1,164.50 to produce an engraved adaptation of the Carpenter painting—not including a $500 fee to Carpenter himself.[36] The print (Fig. 86) was successful enough, but by appearing so late (1867) Carpenter's picture, formed around the same pose of Lincoln and Tad that everyone else by then was using, lost the distinction of having originated the domestic Lincoln. Yet Carpenter almost surely did so, the sitting which produced the Lincoln and Tad and some eight other photographs having been taken in Carpenter's presence. As a painter, Carpenter was too slavish in his copying, too slow, and too reluctant to obey his first pictorial impulses (revisions nearly always made his portraits worse). But he had a feeling for the pulse of the age, having a major hand in creating the public image of Lincoln as the Great Emancipator and the private image of Lincoln as the gentle father with his little son. Lincoln's willingness to have Carpenter underfoot in the White House for months was eventually well recompensed.

As a model for nearly all the family portraits, the printmakers seized on the Lincoln and Tad photograph, combining it with individual images of Mrs. Lincoln and the other boys (occasionally turning one boy's head away from the viewer if a photograph of him were not readily available as a model). Frequently, the youngest child's clothing was copied from a European domestic print and appeared quite improbably dandified and sissified for the railsplitter's parlor. And for some reason, printmakers often made the unknown child smaller than Tad; Willie was actually older, of course.

What these prints document is the deepest wellsprings of Victorian American feeling rather than the Lincoln family. Sentimentalism, which arose in reaction to the rigors of the Calvinist view of death, especially of infant death, had a firm grip on many American households. It had a particularly tight grip on mothers, most of whom had seen infant mortality firsthand and who, as mistress of the home, probably were responsible for its decoration and bought the prints.[37]

Reliance on such traditional images had grown out of recommendations set forth during the popularization of lithography—a dispensation that gave the print a respected place in the traditional American home. As the Reverend G. W. Bethune said in a lecture delivered before the Artist Fund Society of Philadelphia in 1840:

> The lithograph may be rude and gaudy, cinerary urns be turned into flower vases, goddesses made to hold candles, and cross legged Cupids to read little books; but you will rarely find, in a humble family, a taste for these ornaments unaccompanied by neatness, temperance and thrift. They are like cherished plants in

the window, the green creepers in the yard, or the caged singing bird on the wall, signs of a fondness for home and a desire to cultivate those virtues which make home peaceful and happy.

The blessing of clerics such as Dr. Bethune dovetailed nicely with the growing fashion for decorating homes with prints. The trend would prove obnoxious to some critics, including one writer from *Art Interchange* who would complain, only a few years after Lincoln's death: "There appears to be a prejudice on the part of women, against leaving any considerable portion of the wall space uncovered.... No lithographed advertising plaque is too atrocious in design or coloring to prevent its being used in a beribboned state to disfigure house walls." The author Catherine Beecher was among the more representative observers of her time who insisted that prints, especially those with a historical sense, belonged in the home. "Surrounded by such ... reminders of history and art," she said, "children are constantly trained to correctness of taste and refinement of thought, and stimulated ... to the eager and intelligent inquiry about the scenes, the places, the incidents represented."[38]

Thus blessed, it is not surprising that the family print became one of the most popular art forms of the 1840s, 1850s, and 1860s. Lincoln's death inspired Buttre and Sartain, along with Kurz & Allison of Chicago; Currier & Ives, Moore & Annin, and Robertson, all of New York; the Kelloggs of Hartford; William Smith and Joseph Hoover (Fig. 89) of Philadelphia; and Haskell & Allen (see Fig. 84) of Boston—in fact, all the leading printmakers of the country—to issue variations on the theme.

Some were unobjectionable but uninspired productions; others poorly researched composites, historically worthless. Some

FIGURE 88. Photograph of Lincoln and Tad by Alexander Gardner, Washington, D.C. (probably February 1865). (*Library of Congress*)

FIGURE 89. Anton Hohenstein, *President Lincoln and His Family./Respectfully Dedicated to the People of the United States,* published by Joseph Hoover, Philadelphia (1865). Hand-colored lithograph, 24 ⅜ × 17 ½ in. Based loosely on the 1865 Gardner photograph (Fig. 88), this almost comically malproportioned print reversed the central figures of Lincoln and Tad to disguise the origins of the portraiture. With the addition of an even smaller child figure, however, Tad again is implicitly transformed into his older brother, the late Willie; the drummer boy at left now represents Tad. Lincoln's legs are shortened and his torso enlarged, as if it had been inflated with air. Only the recognizable Gardner studio table remains intact, though it has been cheapened by the addition of a potted plant and inexplicably moved outdoors, where the scene is further cluttered by the awkward imposition of an American flag on a pole and a sailing ship moored in the distance. (*Library of Congress*)

PRESIDENT LINCOLN AND HIS FAMILY.
Respectfully Dedicated to the People of the United States.

had artistic merit. Others were, just as Sartain's circular complained, "cheap" and "inferior." In short, there was something for everyone.

The unskilled crudity of most Lincoln family prints is as much a comment on the public demand for domestic art as on the infant capabilities of America's graphic arts industry. The prints were, typically, long on love and short on technical skill; but they were eloquent testimony to the reverence America held for Abraham Lincoln after his death. And they were probably responsible for developing among Americans a nearly insatiable market for pictures of presidential families, or "First Family" pictures as they eventually came to be called.

Thomas Arnold of Rugby noted "that peculiar sense of solemnity" with which "the very idea of family life was invested" in the Victorian era. The family became, as Walter Houghton points out, a shelter from the anxieties of business and public life and a shelter for those moral and spiritual values at odds with the commercial and political spirit: altruism, religion, and aesthetic culture. After Willie's death, Mary Todd Lincoln chided herself for having "become so wrapped up in the world, so devoted to our own political advancement" that God afflicted them with that deadly reminder of her "worldliness."[39]

Americans did not want worldly and ruthlessly ambitious men in the presidency. They wanted their presidents domesticated. And the printmakers gave them what they wanted. If the President himself failed, as Lincoln did, to get his family together for a picture, the printmakers did it for him.

It is tempting to say that these sentimental domestic images stood, politically, as mute testimony that this warm family man could not possibly be what his political detractors said he was and

MR. LINCOLN. RESIDENCE AND HORSE,

in Springfield, Illinois, as they appeared on his return at the close of the Campaign with Senator Douglas.

FIGURE 90. L[ouis]. Kurz, *Mr. Lincoln. Residence and Horse, In Springfield, Illinois . . . on his return at the close of the Campaign with Senator Douglas,* published by Alfred Storey & Co., Chicago (1865). Lithograph, 20 ¾ × 15 ½ in. The anachronism in this print, showing a bearded Lincoln before his election to the presidency, is perhaps a less important error than the false impression about presidental campaigns it imparts. Lincoln adhered to the view that presidential candidates should not campaign; he never left Springfield for the canvass and therefore could not have returned. This print indicates how strong the symbol of the Lincoln home had become in print portraiture, the hearthstone behind the martyr's greatness. *(Louis A. Warren Lincoln Library and Museum)*

THE HOME OF OUR MARTYRED PRESIDENT

FIGURE 91. [Printmaker unknown], *The Home of Our Martyred President,* (c. 1865). Hand-colored lithograph, 19 ½ × 13 ¾ in. The home portrayed here, despite the claim in its caption, is not Lincoln's frame house but Ashland, Henry Clay's fine brick plantation. The print even includes a picture of Clay in front of his house, as well as slaves and slave cabins, most incongruous for the Great Emancipator. *(Louis A. Warren Lincoln Library and Museum)*

what his assassin believed him truly to be, a tyrant who muzzled the press that criticized him and threw into "American bastilles" anyone who opposed his administration. Yet not a single one of the family prints bears a date before 1865. The quiet power of the family prints to answer political criticism apparently went unrecognized by the politicians. These prints sentimentalized Lincoln's image only after his death. They met a grass-roots need. They were not an invention of the politicians.

The number of Lincoln family prints is legion, and they are reminiscent of the many Washington family prints derived from Edward Savage and David Edwin's *The Washington Family*, produced in 1798. The similarity was hardly accidental. One advertising circular of the period said of Lincoln and Washington: "Every true lover of their deeds, every honest and noble patriot, will be sure to have their Biographies upon their tables, and Engravings of both with their families, of a quality that will equal as near as possible, in exquisite beauty, the sacred deeds of the Father and Savior of our Country. . . ."[40] Indeed, even as the Lincoln family prints began to flood the land in 1865, so did prints of "the father and savior" of the country, initiating a major change in the American pantheon. The association of Washington and Lincoln, however, went back some time.

"The head of Washington hangs in my dining-room . . . and I cannot keep my eyes off of it," Ralph Waldo Emerson had noted in his journal in the summer of 1852.[41] Thousands of Americans were like Emerson in having a Washington print in their homes before the Civil War. As early as 1778, when the outcome of the American Revolution was still far from certain, Washington was already being described as *"Des Landes Vater"* (The Father of His Country) on the illustrated cover of a Pennsylvania German almanac. By then, his transformation "into a national icon" was well under way.[42] Upon his death, he became America's undisputed patron saint. Accordingly, association with Washington came to be welcomed by people in all walks of life, but especially by the managers of the political world. Candidates could always profit by basking in Washington's reflected glory. Abraham Lincoln was no exception.

Lincoln's first "appearance" with Washington had come soon after his nomination in the expensive lithograph by Edward Mendel (Fig. 12). The Chicago artist's work showed a plain and somber Westerner looking at the viewer, with a bust of Washington at his elbow. A day after receiving a copy of the print, Lincoln thanked Mendel for the *"truthful"* image, underlining the key word. Lincoln sent his unusually enthusiastic letter by return mail, and the enterprising artist used it to merchandise his print. Lincoln may have liked the print in part because he liked to see Washington at his elbow. As the stern reality of the presidency loomed ever larger before him, Lincoln developed a new understanding of and appreciation for the first man to hold that office. When Lincoln bade farewell to his neighbors in his little Illinois town, he did so believing that before him was a task "greater than that which rested upon Washington":

My friends—No one, not in my situation, can appreciate my feeling of sadness at this parting. To this place, and the kindness of these people, I owe every thing. Here I have lived a quarter of a century, and have passed from a young to an old man. Here my children have been born, and one is buried. I now leave, not knowing when, or whether ever, I may return, with a task before me greater than that which rested upon Washington. Without the

PRESIDENT LINCOLN AND FAMILY CIRCLE.

FIGURE 92. Lyon & Co., *President Lincoln and Family Circle. / To the friends of universal freedom and equal rights for all, this picture is respectfully dedicated by the publisher,* New York (1867). Lithograph, 23 ¾ × 17 ½ in. In this stately reworking of several old photographs, including the Lincoln and Tad pose by Gardner (Fig. 88) and the 1864 Lincoln portrait by Brady (Fig. 70), the Lincolns are portrayed inside the White House, a huge oval portrait of Washington dominating the scene and making an unmistakable connection between the two national heroes portrayed. Note the recurring accessories: a flag, this time held by the youngest child; the decorative floral arrangement, signifying the comforts of home; Robert in uniform, reminding viewers of his military service during the war; and the tranquil scene outside, representing the peace made possible under Lincoln's leadership. *(Louis A. Warren Lincoln Library and Museum)* assistance of that Divine Being, who ever attended him, I cannot succeed. With that assistance I cannot fail. Trusting in Him, who can go with me, and remain with you and be every where for good, let us confidently hope that all will yet be well. To His care commending you, as I hope in your prayers you will commend me, I bid you an affectionate farewell.[43]

God, Washington, friends—a truly troubled Lincoln spoke from the heart. He had briefly dropped his guard of humility and spoken in a way that made him potentially greater than the "Father of His Country"—provided he succeeded at the "task before me."[44]

Some have argued that this view may have preceded the crisis of 1861. Psychohistorians have detected a tiny flame of adult desire to be as great as Washington as early as 1838 in Lincoln's now famed Lyceum speech. These scholars see Washington and Lincoln as rivals in the ages-old conflict between fathers and sons, Lincoln and others like him feeling that the founders preempted the field of historical glory and left little room for great deeds by their ambitious sons.[45]

Whatever tension there was between Washington's generation and Lincoln's, it was well hidden behind abundant expressions of filial piety. Lincoln shared this reverence with his generation. "Washington . . . is the mightiest name of earth," he said on Washington's Birthday in 1842. "On that name, an eulogy is expected. It cannot be. To add brightness to the sun, or glory to the name of Washington, is alike impossible. Let none attempt it. In solemn awe pronounce the name, and in its naked deathless splendor, leave it shining on."[46] As President, Lincoln was still thinking about "our fathers" at Gettysburg in 1863. Although

Lincoln never wrote, as Emerson did, about a Washington portrait in his dining room, printmakers who showed Lincoln's dining room exactly that way (see Fig. 92) took justifiable artistic liberties.

Lincoln revered Washington but, as a good politician, he also used him. He most frequently associated his name with Washington's in the same manner most politicians did. "The Republicans are walking in the 'old paths,' " those of Washington and the other founders, Lincoln argued again and again in the 1850s. At the Cooper Union in New York early in 1860, he defended himself against opponents who were "imploring men to unsay what Washington said, and undo what Washington did." If in the decade before the Civil War he turned Washington into something of an antislavery champion and thereby a spiritual ancestor of the Republicans, during the two preceding decades he had invoked Washington's name with equal fervor on behalf of his Whiggish economic policies. Lincoln and the printmakers alike were attempting to add the glory of old to his name by the association.[47]

But if the Father's image could be invoked to show that the sons were walking in his footsteps, the opposite effect was also attainable. Just before Lincoln's first inauguration, a woodcut in *Harper's Weekly* pictured the incoming President and his future Secretary of State, William H. Seward, looking on piously while abolitionist preacher Henry Ward Beecher refused communion to a kneeling George Washington (Fig. 93). The cartoon carried an abolitionist slogan as its caption: "No Communion with Slaveholders." A similar critical message could be conveyed by substituting for America's patron saint the image of a figure that evoked hostile feelings. Thus Adalbert Volck's Emancipation Proclama-

NO COMMUNION WITH SLAVEHOLDERS.
"Stand aside, you Old Sinner! WE are HOLIER than thou!"

FIGURE 93. [Printmaker unknown], *No Communion with Slaveholders./"Stand aside, you Old Sinner! WE are HOLIER than thou!"* published in *Harper's Weekly* (March 2, 1861). Included for its interesting reference to Washington and Lincoln, this woodcut was not a separately printed image but stemmed from that other great source of illustrations in Lincoln's era, the New York illustrated newspapers. *(Louis A. Warren Lincoln Library and Museum)*

FIGURE 94. Currier & Ives, *Washington and Lincoln./The Father and the Saviour of Our Country,* New York (1865). Colored lithograph, 11 × 14 ⅞ in. The Lincoln portrait is based on a Brady studio photograph (Fig. 70). *(Harry T. Peters Collection, Museum of the City of New York)*

tion etching had included above Lincoln's head the framed portrait of "St. Ossawotamie"—a murderous John Brown—exactly where the pro-Lincoln artist would have placed Washington's portrait (Fig. 61).

After Lincoln's assassination, picture publishers began to point toward Lincoln's emergence as a national saint in his own right, transforming the Washington-Lincoln relationship in prints and photographic composites—and in the consciousness of Americans.[48] *Liberty Crowning Its Martyr,* a composite *carte-de-visite,* elevated Lincoln to a new height, with the classical goddess of Liberty placing a crown upon the kneeling Lincoln. Her right hand bestowed the crown of laurels and her left hand the traditional staff, her arm resting on a bust of Washington.

Washington and Lincoln also appeared next to each other as equals or near equals. The many examples indicate the grassroots demand for Washington-Lincoln prints generated by John Wilkes Booth's act. The unscrupulous printmakers, or those merely in a great hurry who reworked their own creations, bur-

WASHINGTON AND LINCOLN.
THE FATHER AND THE SAVIOUR OF OUR COUNTRY.

nished out the heads of the great men of earlier days and replaced them with Lincoln's head, as in the *Union* print (Figs. 34, 35), and added a figure of Washington.

Currier & Ives's *Washington and Lincoln,/The Father and the Saviour of Our Country,* showed the eternal flame of liberty with an American eagle and shield in the background (Fig. 94). Lincoln's left hand held a document, presumably the Emancipation Proclamation, providing pictorial proof that the President's twin claims to fame were immediately recognized: he saved the Union and abolished slavery. The artist chose to portray Washington in eighteenth- and Lincoln in nineteenth-century dress. The composition granted Washington a slight superiority not only by the anointing motion of his left hand but also by making him a trifle taller than Lincoln (in real life it was the other way around). The symbolic significance of this difference in height was all the more noteworthy because Lincoln's tall frame had become one of his most distinguishing characteristics. The artist was intent on showing the Father superior to the Saviour.

The Washington-Lincoln prints that portrayed only the busts or heads of the two heroes eroded the sense of hierarchical difference between the two men. These double portraits thus help measure Lincoln's rise toward equality with Washington. *Columbia's Noblest Sons* by Kimmel & Forster illustrates this trend well (Fig. 95). The lithographers strengthened the suggestion of equal rank by including around the border of the print vignettes of important moments from the Revolution and the Civil War. Washington was flanked by images of the Boston Tea Party, the signing of the Declaration of Independence, and the British surrender at Yorktown; Lincoln, by images of the bombardment of Fort Sumter, the battle between the *Monitor* and the *Merrimack,*

Columbia= noblest Sons

FIGURE 95. Kimmel & Forster, *Columbia's noblest Sons*, copyrighted by Henry and William Vought, and published by Manson Lang, New York (1865). Lithograph, 19 ¼ × 13 ½ in. This is perhaps the typical Washington-Lincoln print, Columbia crowning the founder and preserver of the Union with twin laurel wreaths. Beneath the cameo portraits, the guns of war are stilled and the symbolic shackles of slavery broken. Kimmel & Forster issued an identically designed print depicting Lincoln with Grant in which, unaccountably, Columbia appeared partially undraped. *(Louis A. Warren Lincoln Library and Museum)*

ABRAHAM LINCOLN, THE MARTYR
VICTORIOUS

and Lincoln's entrance into Richmond. Below Washington the artists placed the Declaration of Independence; below Lincoln, the Emancipation Proclamation. The meaning was unmistakable: the birth of freedom in America under Washington in 1776 and the "new birth of freedom" on January 1, 1863, were of equal importance. Liberty's right foot, next to Washington, rested on the British lion. Next to Lincoln, the American eagle emerged behind her left foot. Her symmetrically outstretched arms placed laurel wreaths simultaneously on the brows of the two presidents. No wonder some went so far as to believe that the "son," Lincoln, was descended from the seed biological of the Father, Washington.[49]

The combination of the religious with the patriotic—part of a phenomenon that some scholars describe as "civil religion"—was most obvious in the apotheosis prints that showed Washington's welcoming Lincoln into heaven. The heaven depicted was a symbolic Mount Olympus to many printmakers, a Christian heaven to most of the viewing public, and a confused combination to yet others (including some printmakers). In John Sartain's print, Washington and Lincoln embraced upon their meeting in the clouds while angels played the harp, prayed, held an olive branch over Washington, and placed laurel on Lincoln (Fig. 96).

In the classical art of antiquity, apotheosis depicted the exaltation of a mortal to the company of the gods. In Christian art, the Resurrection usually included soldiers asleep before the sarcophagus, with Christ rising from it in a winding sheet. The Renaissance began to combine the two afterworlds, and the baroque heaven came to be much like Mount Olympus.[50] Sartain's *Abraham Lincoln, the Martyr Victorious* nicely showed the eclectic nature

FIGURE 96. John Sartain after a design by W. H. Hermans, *Abraham Lincoln, The Martyr./Victorious.* Published by W. H. Hermans, Penn Yan, Yates County, New York (1865). Engraving, 13 7/8 × 18 1/8 in. *(Louis A. Warren Lincoln Library and Museum)*

of America's heaven. So did D. T. Wiest's *In Memory of Abraham Lincoln.*

The origins of Wiest's lithograph reached back over half a century to a few days before Christmas 1800, when John James Barralet invited the public to view a nearly completed print:

> The subject—General Washington raised from the tomb, by the spiritual and temporal Genius—assisted by Immortality. At his feet America weeping over his Armour, holding the staff surmounted by the Cap of Liberty, emblematical of his mild administration, on the opposite side, an Indian crouched in surly sorrow. In the third ground the mental virtues, Faith, Hope, and Charity.[51]

Barralet was Americanizing age-old European traditions (Fig. 97). An Indian, the European symbol of the Western Hemisphere, mourned in the foreground of the print together with the goddess of Liberty, in the eyes of Americans more and more America itself. At her feet were the armor of a knight, symbolic of Washington's military prowess; *fasces,* or a bundle of rods, the ancient Roman emblem of power that had come to stand for the unity and lawful force of the new nation; and snakes, probably meant to represent the evil subdued by Liberty and the American eagle. The bowed figure of the Indian and Liberty were in poses quite like the sleeping soldiers of Resurrection scenes.

The American eagle was next to Liberty. The left background contained what Barralet's advertisement called "the mental virtues, Faith, Hope, and Charity," the somewhat domesticated and Protestantized versions of old Christian virtues. Faith leaned on the cross, Hope (rather like a nun in appearance) looked heaven-

FIGURE 97. John James Barralet, *Apotheosis of George Washington,* published by Simon Chaudron and Barralet, Philadelphia, (January 1802). Stipple engraving, 18 ½ × 24 in. *(Library of Congress)*

ward, and Charity suckled her babes as in countless European works.

Washington, in winding robes, ascended from his tomb amid clouds into a beam of light. "Immortality" and "the spiritual and temporal Genius" (according to Barralet's original anouncement, but "Poetical and Historical Genius," according to a later advertisement)[52] assisted Washington. The bearded old man with wings (with the symbols of death—a scythe and an hourglass—beside him) was the centuries-old figure of Father Time.

Over the years the *Apotheosis of George Washington* (Fig. 97) was reengraved and republished several times and appeared on canvas and crockery as well as in other mediums. Then in 1865 it underwent an all-important transformation. Wiest replaced Washington's face with Lincoln's, changed the name on the tomb, and issued the lithograph *In Memory of Abraham Lincoln—The Reward of the Just* (Fig. 98).

The print pirate wasted no time or effort in getting "his" work before the public. Incongruities abounded in it. Although Lincoln had just led the nation through four years of bloody war to keep all the states of the Union together, the American shield in the print bore only fifteen stars, corresponding to the number of states in Washington's Republic. Although Lincoln spent most of his life in the Whig party, which included the old Anti-Masons among its number, the emblem of the Freemasons now hung from his tomb. The badge of the Society of the Cincinnati, an organization of Army officers to which Washington had belonged, appeared in the print, but Lincoln's brief and somewhat farcical service in the Black Hawk War hardly qualified him either for that or for the symbolic armor. Others may have wondered about the mourning Indian; a freed black man would have been far more

FIGURE 98. D. T. Wiest, *In Memory of Abraham Lincoln—The Reward of the Just,* published by William Smith, Philadelphia (1865). Lithograph, 18 ⅜ × 24 in. For this apotheosis print, Lincoln's head is substituted for Washington's; otherwise the scene remains substantially the same Lincoln's head is based on the popular 1864 photogarph (Fig. 45). (*Louis A. Warren Lincoln Library and Museum*)

appropriate. But Wiest knew that he could get away with his clumsy piracy.

In the early 1800s, Barralet's engraving probably aimed at a small, rather elite market in a nation of less than six million people. For an elite educated in classical traditions, the imagery of the print, one suspects, was reasonably clear. The nation, however, changed over the years.

By 1865, it had grown much larger, to around thirty-six million. As learning became more democratized and widespread, classical, humanistic, and European religious imagery had at best a tenuous place. Yet art came to be in ever greater demand, especially art by the people and for the people. The nation grew wealthier, too, and an inexpensive lithograph that captured the imagination could also capture large audiences. It is a fair guess that Barralet's engraving—its six states notwithstanding—sold fewer copies than Wiest's lithograph. It did not matter that much whether the symbolism was wrong for a Lincoln print. People no longer knew.

Nor did they know that in one respect the allegory created for Washington was superbly right for Lincoln. Liberty held in her hand the ancient symbols of freedom: the *uindicata*, or *festuca*, and the *pilleus*. The former was a staff, the rod that the ancient Roman judge laid upon a slave who was being freed; the latter was the skullcap given to freedmen to announce their new status.[53] For the Great Emancipator's apotheosis, these symbols were altogether fitting.

Wiest's work also pointed to the future. In substituting Lincoln's head for Washington's, the printmaker, like an unwitting weathercock, marked the direction of the winds of history. The universal tendency to exaggerate the importance of the contemporary historical moment, combined with the momentous events of war and assassination, helped in 1865 to elevate the sixteenth President close to the heights of the first in public esteem. Yet with the exception of the freed slaves, who worshipped Lincoln as no others did, and the majority of Southern whites, who detested him, Americans for a generation or more continued to rank Washington "first in the hearts of his countrymen." He now had a rival; but, on the whole, the two giants stood near each other with no peers in sight.

Late in the century, for example, John T. Morse, Jr., the editor of the popular "American Statesman" series of biographies, decided that only Lincoln and Washington merited treatment at two-volume length, and Morse rated Washington the greater of the two men.[54] Theodore Roosevelt, one of Morse's authors, could still declare early in the twentieth century that "Washington was, not even excepting Lincoln, the very greatest man of modern times." Yet even as Roosevelt's presidency drew to its end and the nation celebrated the centennial of Lincoln's birth, change in Lincoln's stature measured the change of American values. Roosevelt's word "modern" continued its inevitable transmogrification, and the sixteenth President came to be more representative of modernity than the first. The son moved ahead of the Father.

The two leaders continued to stand next to each other decade after decade in twentieth-century polls of historians, but their previous rankings were reversed. Then, in a poll of historians taken in 1982, Washington for the first time slipped to third place behind Franklin Delano Roosevelt. But Lincoln's position remained unchanged. History in the end justified Wiest's piracy.[55]

Lincoln had revered "our fathers," as he called them, but he could also scoff at the idealization of historical heroes, at apotheoses—even of Washington. In the White House soon after his first inauguration, Lincoln related with relish an anecdote about Ohio Senator Thomas Corwin, who had been told by an old man in Virginia who knew Washington that George Washington often swore. Corwin's father had always held up the father of his country as a faultless person, and told his son to follow in his footsteps.

"Well," said Corwin, "when I heard that George Washington was addicted to the vices and infirmities of man, I felt so relieved that I just shouted for joy."[56]

Lincoln told the story with a hearty laugh. He could wear the mantle of his predecessor lightly—like some of the printmakers. He was egalitarian to the bone and could be completely at ease in the company of a former slave, but he likewise had little difficulty seeing himself as the equal of the Father of the country. On the frontier where he grew up, one of the ultimate equalizers was physical strength, especially as utilized in wrestling. Once when President Lincoln was told of Washington's reputation as a great wrestler, Lincoln brought up his own fame in such matters, and added: "If George was loafing around here now, I should be glad to have a tussle with him, and I rather believe that one of the plain people of Illinois would be able to manage the aristocrat of Old Virginia."[57]

The Lincoln-Washington portraits as well as the family scenes show that an abundance of outright fakery found its way into the marketplace. Printmakers, facing the greatest public demand yet for the portraits of Lincoln and keen competition for original designs and sales, occasionally resorted to the wildest chicanery to bring out products quickly. In the clamor for "new" images, expedience dictated that a number of retouched variants, mirror-image piracies, and other fakes and thefts be rushed to the public before some of the better works could be produced.

A number of printmakers reissued their old beardless lithographs and engravings of Lincoln the candidate. These had been updated once to reflect Lincoln's decision to grow a beard back in 1861. Now, black borders and reverential captions were added to update them yet again. It did not seem to matter that Lincoln had aged so much during his presidency that to many observers he no longer resembled the man portrayed in such prints.

Faced with the large demand for Lincoln pictures and an overstock of long-outdated plates of historical figures from the generation past, some printmakers dusted off such plates, burnished out the old heads, and added Lincoln's face to whatever physique was in their possession. Eager to reap the financial rewards of rushing Lincoln portraits to market, such image-makers haphazardly joined Lincoln's countenance to such unlikely figures as Martin Van Buren (the shortest President), the diminutive Francis Preston Blair, Jr., (Figs. 99, 100), the dashing John C. Frémont, and Andrew Jackson.[58]

The printmakers did, in all fairness, face a dilemma. The last photographs of the living Lincoln—the 1865 poses by Alexander Gardner and Henry Warren[59]—showed a Lincoln so painfully, uncharacteristically thin that few engravers or lithographers dared copy them as models for their "martyr" prints. Most portraitists resolutely refused to record the physical consequences of the Lincoln presidency on its chief executive, for as a martyr, they probably reasoned, he should not appear wasted or even haggard. Part of the dying-god legend required that its heroes be struck down in their prime. So printmakers romanticized Lincoln's features in their post-assassination portrayals, making his

FIGURE 99. A PRINT OF FRANCIS PRESTON BLAIR, JR., . . .
(Library of Congress)

. . . REEMERGES AS A "NEW" PRINT OF LINCOLN.

FIGURE 100. John Sartain, [*Lincoln*], published by R. R. Landon, Chicago (*c.* 1865). Hand-colored mezzotint engraving, 21 ½ × 15 in. This is one of several composite prints issued after Lincoln's assassination for which slightly unscrupulous engravers adapted outdated portraits of former or less saleable celebrities by substituting Lincoln's head. Blair's paunch is inappropriate, and his fine hands never split rails. (*Louis A. Warren Lincoln Library and Museum*)

now-gaunt physique heroic rather than taking the commercial risk required to reveal the truth.

The truth was all too visible to those who observed Lincoln at first hand. John Hay had noted the change in passing judgment on the two life masks of Lincoln, the first made by Leonard W. Volk shortly before Lincoln's nomination as President in 1860, the second made by Clark Mills near the time of the President's fifth-sixth birthday, in 1865. Wrote Hay:

> The first is of a man of fifty-one, and young for his years. The face has a clean, firm outline; it is free from fat, but the muscles are hard and full; the large mobile mouth is ready to speak, to shout, or laugh; the bold curved nose is substantial, with spreading nostrils; it is a face full of life, of energy, of vivid aspiration. The other is so sad and peaceful in its infinite repose. . . . The lines are set, as if the living face, like the copy, had been in bronze; the nose is thin, and lengthened by the emaciation of the cheeks; the mouth is fixed like that of an archaic statue; a look as of one on whom sorrow and care had done their worst without victory . . . the whole expression is of unspeakable sadness.[60]

But this was not the Lincoln whom the printmakers chose to portray. Americans, like Walt Whitman, were asking:

> O what shall I hang on the chamber walls?
> And what shall the pictures be that I hang on the walls,
> To adorn the burial-house of him I love?[61]

They would hang pictures of the martyr at the peak of his powers, as he looked when he issued the Emancipation Proclamation, as printmakers assumed he had looked during his days as a lawyer and campaigner in Illinois: images that had little basis in fact but reflected much reverence and goodwill.

One scene of his murder was captioned:

This Lincoln
Hath borne his faculties so meek; has been
So clear in his great office; that his virtues
Shall plead, trumped-tongued [sic], against
The deep damnation of his taking off.[62]

The portraiture was so rudimentary in some prints that such devices as captioned "poetry" offered yet another "art" with which to honor Lincoln. The poetry quoted below *The Martyr of Liberty* (Fig. 76) was better than most, as it was adapted from *Macbeth*—an appropriate device for a lover of Shakespeare like Lincoln. But the better "martyr" portraits required no such embellishment.

One of the best of the straightforward, elegant post-assassination Lincoln prints was the large-sized work that has come to be known as the "Littlefield Engraving." In reality, it was the work of engraver Henry Gugler, who used a "cartoon" by John H. Littlefield (*b.* 1835) as the model (Fig. 101).

Littlefield had known Lincoln in his youth. Born in Cicero, Illinois, in 1835, he had learned carriage-making from his father, who soon recognized his artistic ability and promoted him to the design department of his factory. The family moved to Grand Rapids, Michigan, where John took up the study of law. In 1858, Littlefield's brother met Lincoln in Ottawa, Illinois, and asked him to consider John for a place as a student in the Lincoln-Herndon law firm. Lincoln agreed to "take a look at him."

Littlefield apparently remained attached to the law office until Lincoln's inauguration as President in 1861, but he soon forsook the legal profession for a career in art, his first love. Though Lincoln may have secured for him a patronage job in the Treasury Department, the artist's reminiscences do not include evidence that he saw or sketched Lincoln during his presidency. All that is known is that after the assassination, Littlefield produced a death-bed scene. Later, he decided to do a large overall portrait, modeled after the Brady photograph now used on the five-dollar bill. A few years thereafter, a newspaper reported that the painting was finally "being engraved in pure line, the size of life. . . . Those who have seen the portrait pronounced it a superb work of art." "I organized the Lincoln publishing Co. for the purpose of engraving this cartoon," Littlefield remembered, ". . . with a capital of $11,000." He would pay an engraver $3,500 annually for three years to do the job.[63]

The printmaker commissioned for the task of engraving the painting was Henry Gugler (1816–1880), a German-born banknote engraver who probably made Littlefield's acquaintance when the painter worked at the Treasury. Gugler was employed at the National Note Bureau, where he engraved vignette portraits for American currency.[64] His adaptation of the Littlefield was considered his finest work: a life-sized print, the finished plate for which was advertised at the time of its first printings to be worth $10,000. In later years, Gugler founded a lithographic firm in Milwaukee, though he never again executed a commission as famous as Littlefield's Lincoln.[65] As for Littlefield himself, he went on the lecture circuit, where he prospered for years, much in demand to speak on his principal topic: Abraham Lincoln.

A competitive portrait was the work of William Edgar Marshall

FIGURE 101. Henry Gugler after a painting by John H. Littlefield, *Lincoln.* Published by William Pate & Co., New York (1869). Engraving, 23 × 29 ¼ in. Gugler worked for three years on this elephant folio reproduction of Littlefield's "cartoon," which the artist later claimed was the largest Lincoln line portrait ever engraved on steel. It had been based on the Brady five-dollar bill photograph (Fig. 45). Charles Sumner told Littlefield: "Our martyred President lives in this engraving." A limited run of signed India proofs sold for the astonishing price of $100. (quoted in Littlefield "Statement," Oct. 8, 1875, in the New-York Historical Society. Although Littlefield had known Lincoln in Illinois when he worked as a law student in the Lincoln-Herndon office, he based his painting entirely on the Brady five-dollar-bill photograph (Fig. 45). *(Louis A. Warren Lincoln Library and Museum)*

(1837–1906). A New York–born painter and engraver who had started his career when still a teenager by engraving decorative pocketwatch covers, Marshall studied in France under Thomas Couture during the Civil War. Returning in 1865, he took on the Lincoln project. The result was a painting, and a subsequent print adaptation, whose fame would guarantee Marshall a constant, lucrative flow of portrait commissions for the remaining forty years of his life. The print would even be displayed in the home of Frederick Douglass.[66]

Couture himself thought Marshall's solemn painting of Lincoln "superb, striking, and fine, admirable in color." In late 1866 the Boston firm of Ticknor & Fields announced that they had "arranged with the eminent engraver and painter, Mr. Wm. E. Marshall, for the publication of his line engraved portrait of Abraham Lincoln." Boasted the circular: "It is the largest head ever engraved in this manner, and is by far the best engraving ever executed in America, and will take its place among the few great works which lineal art has given to the world." Moreover, the publishers promised, "it will be accepted as the standard portrait of Mr. Lincoln" (Fig. 102).

Critics reacted most favorably to the published print. Writing in the *Atlantic Monthly,* one critic called it "beyond question the finest instance of line-engraving yet executed on this continent." And Gustave Doré, the French illustrator, termed it "the best engraving ever made by any artist living or dead."

Ticknor & Fields sent proof copies of Marshall's print to several people who had known Lincoln intimately, and they, too, responded with enthusiastic endorsements, which were published in the firm's 1866 circular. Robert Todd Lincoln, for example, testified to "its excellence as a likeness," adding: "I cannot sug-

FIGURE 102. William Edgar Marshall, *Abraham Lincoln,* published by Ticknor & Fields, Boston, and by Marshall (1866). Engraving, 16 × 20 ¾ in. Historian George Bancroft predicted that the Marshall engraving "will be sought for two hundred years hence, and every collection of American engravings that is without it will be considered imperfect." So far, Bancroft has proven substantially correct. (*Louis A. Warren Lincoln Library and Museum*)

ABRAHAM LINCOLN

gest any improvement." William H. Herndon wrote: "If art is the expression of an idea embodied in fact . . . then this picture is a work of the highest art. . . . Those who never had the pleasure of seeing the original may rest assured that the expression of organ and feature and mood of the man are well caught, expressed and observed." It was a *Lincoln,* said Herndon, "in kindness, tenderness and reflection combined. . . ."

To Edwin M. Stanton, the engraving was "a beautiful likeness," representing Lincoln's "living expression with more accuracy than any other that has come under my observation." Added the former Secretary of War: "As one who knew and loved him, I rejoice that you have so well succeeded in your effort, by a work of art, in preserving the memory of his countenance, and enabling the world to know what manner of man he was."

Other laudatory appraisals came from Charles Sumner, who thought the picture captured Lincoln "in his most interesting expression, where gentleness and sympathy unite in strength," and from Speaker of the House Schuyler Colfax, who added that Marshall's *Lincoln* portrayed the late President the way he appeared "when he was calm but grave." This, Colfax thought, was just how Lincoln had looked "the evening before the Inauguration Ball of 1865, when the Rebel armies were still in the field, and he spoke so sadly of the long years and bloody sacrifices of the war, and yet so hopefully of the success he was certain Providence had in store for us."[67]

Only Francis B. Carpenter dissented. Asking for an endorsement of his own Lincoln "martyr" print (an inferior engraving by Frederick W. Halpin of one of Carpenter's White house studies), Carpenter reproached Colfax for his published endorsement of the Marshall print and asked for the Speaker's endorsement for his own effort. Carpenter pointed out that "Marshall's portrait was made up from photographs. MR. LINCOLN *never sat* to him." But generally there was little disagreement at the time that Marshall had produced one of the best print portraits of Lincoln.[68]

As the extraordinarily dignified Lincolns of Littlefield and Marshall and the public reaction to them indicate, the deification of Lincoln was inexorably underway. It was the handsome Lincoln of the artists that the American people would henceforward see.

In truth, however, prints had not really succeeded in capturing Abraham Lincoln in the endless variety of moods his contemporaries described in their written reminiscences; no medium had. The "flexible face" of which Schuyler Colfax wrote and which artists of the period later admitted they found so difficult to portray, remained—and still remains—an enigma. His photographs do not show the real Lincoln, and neither do his paintings or sculpture from life. At best, each medium succeeded in capturing only a part of the living man: photographs, the frozen expression required by the primitive camera; the fine arts, the formal, rigid dignity dictated by artistic convention; and print portraits, the Lincoln "for the people"—more active, more romanticized, more colorful than in any other medium, though also necessarily far less accurate. None had completely captured the man whom observers found at once homely and captivating. As Whitman wrote:

Probably the reader has seen physiognomies (often old farmers, sea captains, and such) that, behind their homeliness, or even ugliness, held superior points so subtle, yet so palpable, making the real life of their faces almost as impossible to depict as a wild perfume or fruit-taste, or a passionate tone of the living voice—and such was Lincoln's face, the peculiar color, the lines of it, the eyes, the mouth, expression. Of technical beauty it had nothing—but to the eye of a great artist it furnished a rare study, a feast and fascination.[69]

In a sense, though, the printmakers had not failed. They had introduced Lincoln to millions of Americans; made his unconventional appearance palatable; helped create an image for him of honesty, patriotism, and strength; chronicled his changing appearance as he headed for the White House; commemorated his war and his decision to emancipate the slaves; and ultimately provided a visual accompaniment to an emerging folklore. The Lincoln they helped chisel into America's increasingly pictorial consciousness was inseparable from the nation he helped preserve.

Printmakers succeeded in chronicling and influencing Lincoln's metamorphosis from virtuous politician to demigod. Though sentiment more often than not took precedence over accuracy, printmakers identified a broad audience in the America of the 1860s and met that audience's needs. What was said of him in one of his funeral orations could have been said of the bulk of Lincoln prints produced in 1865 and after: "There he sleeps, peacefully embalmed in his country's tears."[70]

NOTES

Introduction: *BY THE PEOPLE, FOR THE PEOPLE*

1. Tyler Dennett, ed., *Lincoln and the Civil War in the Diaries and Letters of John Hay* (New York: Dodd, Mead & Co., 1939), p. 143.
2. Philip M. Bikle Typescript, notarized February 12, 1926, Civil War Collections, Gettysburg College Library.
3. *Ibid.*
4. Charles Henry Hart, *A Catalogue of a Collection of Engraved and Other Portraits of Lincoln . . .* (New York: [Grolier Club], 1899); Winfred Porter Truesdell, *Engraved and Lithographed Portraits of Abraham Lincoln* (Champlain, N.Y.: Troutsdale Press, 1933).

Part I "*INTRODUCING A RAIL OLD WESTERN GENTLEMAN*"

1. "Lincoln's Picture," *Campaign Plain Dealer and Popular Sovereignty Advocate*, September 22, 1860, p. 4 (fascimile published at Lincoln, Ill., by Lincoln College, 1960). William E. Baringer's "Campaign Technique in Illinois—1860," in *Transactions of the Illinois State Historical Society for 1931—Publication No. 39* (n.p., n.d.), p. 263, notes the use of the poem as a song.
2. Baringer refers to politics as "the national sport" in a time when life was "hard and monotonous . . . and opportunities for excitement and social intercourse were few, and therefore valued highly" ("Campaign Technique in Illinois—1860," pp. 212, 246). See also Richard P. McCormick, *The Second American Party System: Party Formation in the Jacksonian Era* (Chapel Hill, N.C.: University of North Carolina Press, 1966), pp. 349–350. (Americans "eagerly assumed the identity of

partisans," McCormick says, "perhaps for much the same reason that their descendants were to become Dodger fans.") *Harper's Weekly*'s comment appeared in the issue of June 16, 1860, p. 370. Lincoln's letter is in Roy P. Basler, *et al.*, eds., *The Collected Works of Abraham Lincoln* (9 vols., New Brunswick, N.J.: Rutgers University Press, 1953–55; cited hereafter as *Coll. Works of Lincoln*), III, 37.
3. David M. Potter used the phrase a "hurrah" campaign in *The Impending Crisis, 1848–1861*, completed and edited by Don E. Fehrenbacher (New York: Harper & Row, 1976), p. 434. Baringer borrows the "hullabaloo" term in "Campaign Technique in Illinois—1860," p. 222. G. S. Boritt details Lincoln's early insistence on issues in *Lincoln and the Economics of the American Dream* (Memphis, Tenn.: Memphis State University Press, 1978), pp. 64, 76–78. *Coll. Works of Lincoln*, I, 491. The shrewd Democratic view appeared in the *Campaign Plain Dealer and Popular Sovereignty Advocate*, July 21, 1860, p. 4. Ronald Formisano is quoted in Roger A. Fischer, "The Republican Presidential Campaigns of 1856 and 1860: Analysis Through Artifacts," *Civil War History*, XXVII (June 1981), 123.
4. "The Illinois Scrapbook," *Journal of the Illinois State Historical Society*, XLI (September 1948), 310; William Hanley Smith, "Old-Time Campaigning and the Story of a Lincoln Campaign Song," *Journal of the Illinois State Historical Society*, XIII (April 1920), 24, 31.
5. Chevalier is quoted in John Niven, *Gideon Welles: Lincoln's Secretary of the Navy* (New York: Oxford University Press, 1973), p. 34; Robert Philippe, *Political Graphics: Art as a Weapon* (New York: Abbeville Press, 1980), p. 172.
6. *Coll. Works of Lincoln*, IV, 39.
7. *Ibid.*, IV, 44.
8. *Ibid.*, IV, 45.
9. *Ibid.*, IV, 47, 34.

10. *Ibid.*, IV, 36.
11. William B. Hesseltine, ed., *Three Against Lincoln: Murat Halstead Reports the Caucuses of 1860* (Baton Rouge, La.: Louisiana State University Press, 1960), pp. 143, 144.
12. Louis A. Warren, "The Shower of Lincoln Prints at the Wigwam," *Lincoln Lore*, no. 1044 (April 1949).
13. Herbert Mitgang, ed., *Abraham Lincoln: A Press Portrait* (Chicago: Quadrangle Books, 1971; orig. pub. as *Lincoln As They Saw Him*, New York: Rinehart, 1956), p. 168.
14. From the Curtis copy of the Wigwam engraving in the Louis A. Warren Lincoln Library and Museum, Fort Wayne, Indiana.
15. Allen Thorndike Rice, ed., *Reminiscences of Abraham Lincoln by Distinguished Men of His Time* (New York: North American Review, 1888), p. 593.
16. Warren, "The Shower of Lincoln Prints" and "The Vice-Presidency Twice Beckons Lincoln," *Lincoln Lore*, no. 1646 (April 1975).
17. Mitgang, *Abraham Lincoln: A Press Portrait*, pp. 171, 172, 173; Hesseltine, *Three Against Lincoln*, p. 172.
18. Mitgang, *Abraham Lincoln: A Press Portrait*, p. 172; Francis Bicknell Carpenter, *Six Months at the White House with Abraham Lincoln* (New York: Hurd & Houghton, 1866), p. 46.
19. From an inscription by John G. Nicolay on a second copy of the Wigwam print, also in the Louis A. Warren Lincoln Library and Museum.
20. Mitgang, *Abraham Lincoln: A Press Portrait*, pp. 172, 169, 176, 166.
21. *Ibid.*, pp. 181–182, 185.
22. Robert Gray Gunderson, *The Log-Cabin Campaign* (Lexington, Ky.: University of Kentucky Press, 1957), p. 111; Mitgang, *Abraham Lincoln: A Press Portrait*, pp. 199–200. See also Eric Foner, *Free Soil, Free Labor, Free Men: The Ideology of the Republican Party Before the Civil War* (New York: Oxford University Press, 1970), pp. 11–23,

29–34, and Boritt, *Lincoln and the Economics of the American Dream*, pp. 192–193.
23. *Tazewell County Republican* (Pekin, Ill.), July 13, 1860.
24. Rice, *Reminiscences of Abraham Lincoln*, pp. 480, 479; Osborn H. Oldroyd, ed., *The Lincoln Memorial: Album-Immortelles* (New York: G. W. Carleton, 1883), p. 528; Silas Hawley to George W. Nichols, Oct. 30, 1860, Louis A. Warren Lincoln Library and Museum; Charleston *Mercury* quoted in Wayne C. Williams, *A Rail Splitter for President* (Denver, Col.: University of Denver Press, 1951), p. 144; Boston *Herald*, May 24, 1860, p. 1.
25. Quoted in Mitgang, *Abraham Lincoln: A Press Portrait*, pp. 178–179.
26. Quoted in Frederick Hill Meserve and Carl Sandburg, *The Photographs of Abraham Lincoln* (New York: Harcourt, Brace, 1944), p. 9.
27. Peter Pollack, *The Picture History of Photography* (New York: Harry N. Abrams, 1967), pp. 154–155.
28. Floyd and Marion Rinhart, *The American Daguerreotype* (Athens, Ga.: University of Georgia Press, 1981), pp. 253–254.
29. See William Welling, *Photography in America: The Formative Years, 1839–1900* (New York: Thomas Y. Crowell, 1978), p. 155.
30. Reinhard H. Luthin, *The First Lincoln Campaign* (Cambridge, Mass.: Harvard University Press, 1944), p. 168; Josiah G. Holland, *The Life of Abraham Lincoln* (Springfield, Mass.: Gurdon Bill, 1866), p. 243; Carpenter, *Six Months at the White House*, p. 47.
31. Carpenter, *Six Months at the White House*, p. 47.
32. *Coll. Works of Lincoln*, IV, 89.
33. *Ibid.*, IV, 114.
34. Fischer, "The Republican Presidential Campaigns of 1856 and 1860: Analysis Through Artifacts," p. 131.
35. Mitgang, *Abraham Lincoln: A Press Portrait*, p. 166 (initial capital added); Louis A. Warren, *Lincoln Sheet Music*

Check List (Fort Wayne, Ind.: Lincolniana Publishers, 1940); *Honest Old Abe: Song and Chorus,* Sheet music with words by D. Wentworth (Buffalo, N.Y.: Blodgett & Bradford, 1860).

36. Peter C. Marzio, *The Democratic Art: Pictures for a Nineteenth-Century America* (Boston: David R. Godine, 1979), p. 62. Harry Twyford Peters, *Currier & Ives: Printmakers to the American People* (2 vols., Garden City, N.Y.: Doubleday, Doran, 1929–31), I, 147.

37. Peters, *Currier & Ives,* I, 147.

38. Figures based on Frederic A. Conningham, *Currier & Ives Prints: An Illustrated Check List* (New York: Crown, 1949), *passim.*

39. Stephen Hess and Milton Kaplan, *The Ungentlemanly Art: A History of American Political Cartoons* (rev. ed., New York: Macmillan, 1975), pp. 74–75.

40. The works referred to are James Parton, *Caricature and Other Comic Art . . .* (New York: Harper & Brothers, 1877), p. 324; Arthur Bartless Maurice and Frederic Taber Cooper, *The History of the Nineteenth Century in Caricature* (New York: Dodd, Mead, 1904), pp. 166–167; Allan Nevins and Frank Weitenkampf, *A Century of Political Cartoons* (New York: Charles Scribner's Sons, 1944), pp. 88, 11; Hess and Kaplan, *The Ungentlemanly Art,* pp. 73, 74, 83; and William Murrell, *A History of American Graphic Humor* (2 vols., New York: Whitney Museum of American Art, 1933), p. 238.

41. Hess and Kaplan, *The Ungentlemanly Art,* p. 83; Nevins and Weitenkampf, *A Century of Political Cartoons,* p. 10.

42. Thomas E. Mulligan, Jr., ed., "Hicks Original Believed Found in Copake Home," *New York State and the Civil War,* IV (February 1962), 30; Parke-Bernet Galleries, *Catalogue,* "The Historic First Painting in Oils of Abraham Lincoln," November 23, 1940, p. 1. The catalogue quotes a letter written by Hicks dated January 23, 1879.

43. Holland, *Life of Abraham Lincoln,* p. 233.

44. Rice, *Reminiscences of Lincoln,* pp. 593–599.

45. Earl Schenck Miers, ed., *Lincoln Day by Day: A Chronology, 1809–1865* (3 vols., Washington, D.C.: Lincoln Sesquicentennial Commission, 1960), II, 283; Wilson, *Lincoln in Portraiture,* p. 36.

46. Rice, *Reminiscences of Lincoln,* pp. 602, 606.

47. *Coll. Works of Lincoln,* IV, 75–76.

48. Mulligan, "Hicks Original Believed Found," p. 32; Rice, *Reminiscences of Lincoln,* p. 602.

49. Quoted in Rufus Rockwell Wilson, *Intimate Memories of Lincoln,* (Elmira, N.Y.: Primavera Press, 1945), pp. 308–310.

50. Harold G. and Oswald Garrison Villard, *Lincoln on the Eve of '61: A Journalist's Story by Henry Villard* (New York: Alfred A. Knopf, 1941), p. 36; Boston *Transcript,* July 14, 1860, clipping in the Louis A. Warren Lincoln Library and Museum.

51. Thomas M. Johnston to C. H. Brainard, July 23, 1860, and July 22, 1860, Louis A. Warren Lincoln Library and Museum.

52. Charles A. Barry to George W. Nichols [1860], Louis A. Warren Lincoln Library and Museum; Harry Twyford Peters, *America on Stone* (Garden City, N.Y.: Doubleday, Doran, 1931), p. 87.

53. Marzio, *The Democratic Art,* p. 20.

54. Barry to Nichols [1860]; Silas Hawley to Nichols, October 30, 1860, Louis A. Warren Lincoln Library and Museum; Wilson, *Intimate Memories of Lincoln,* pp. 309–310.

55. Thomas M. Johnston to C. H. Brainard, July 18, 1860, and July 20, 1860, Louis A. Warren Lincoln Library and Museum.

56. C. H. Brainard to Thomas M. Johnston, July 26, 1860 (typed copy), Louis A. Warren Lincoln Library and Museum.

57. Thomas M. Johnston to C. H. Brainard, July 22, 1860; Thomas A. Johnston to David Claypoole Johnston, July 20, 1860, and July 26, 1860, quoted in Boston *Globe,*

February 7, 1932, clipping in Louis A. Warren Lincoln Library and Museum.

58. Henry B. Wehle, *American Miniatures, 1730–1850* (Garden City, N.Y.: Doubleday, 1927), p. 69.

59. John Carlin to William H. Seward, December 26, 1861, Papers of William H. Seward, University of Rochester (microfilm).

60. John G. Nicolay to Therena Bates, August 26, 1860 (typed copy by Helen Nicolay), Louis A. Warren Lincoln Library and Museum.

61. Justin G. and Linda Levitt Turner, *Mary Todd Lincoln: Her Life and Letters* (New York: Alfred A. Knopf, 1972), p. 65; *Coll. Works of Lincoln*, IV, 102; Brown quoted in R. Gerald McMurtry, *Beardless Portraits of Abraham Lincoln Painted from Life* (Fort Wayne, Ind.: Fort Wayne Public Library, 1962), p. 35.

62. John Henry Brown to John G. Nicolay, September 28, 1860, Abraham Lincoln Papers, Library of Congress (microfilm).

63. *Coll. Works of Lincoln*, IV, 127.

64. Silas Hawley to George W. Nichols, October 30, 1860, Louis A. Warren Lincoln Library and Museum; Norman B. Judd to Abraham Lincoln, June 6, 1860, Abraham Lincoln Papers, Library of Congress (microfilm).

65. Quoted in David C. Mearns, *The Lincoln Papers* (2 vols., Garden City, N.Y.: Doubleday, 1948), I, 291–292.

66. Both letters quoted in *Coll. Works of Lincoln*, IV, 129–130.

67. The English engraver D. J. Pound, for one, issued a print called *President Lincoln*, based on Brady's Cooper Institute photograph (Fig. 6), with no beard added. Harold Holzer, "The Bearding of the President, 1860: The Portraitists Put on Hairs," *Lincoln Herald*, LXXVIII (Fall 1976), 99, 101.

68. Paul M. Angle, "Fakery in the Name of Honest Abe," *Chicago History*, IV (1954–55), 47–48.

69. *Coll. Works of Lincoln*, IV, 219.

70. Wilson, *Intimate Memories of Lincoln*, p. 301.

71. The patriotic envelope was by printmaker R. Magee, who described Lincoln as "Uncle Abe" below the small vignette likeness in the upper left-hand corner.

Part II THE ART OF WAR

1. Nathaniel Hawthorne, "Chiefly about War-Matters," *Atlantic Monthly*, X (July 1862), 46.

2. *Harper's Weekly*, November 14, 1863, p. 722.

3. *The American Annual Cyclopaedia and Register of Important Events of the Year 1865* (New York: D. Appleton, 1866), pp. 356, 357.

4. *Harper's Weekly*, May 13, 1865, p. 291; *American Annual Cyclopaedia*, p. 357.

5. *Harper's Weekly*, June 3, 1865, p. 339.

6. Mary A. Livermore, *My Story of the War . . .* (Hartford, Conn.: A. D. Worthington, 1889), pp. 441–442.

7. Charles J. Stillé, *Memorial of the Great Central Fair . . . Held at Philadelphia . . .* (Philadelphia: U.S. Sanitary Commission, 1865), pp. 114–118; *Harper's Weekly*, January 9, 1864, p. 29, April 16, 1864, p. 246; *The Daily Morning Drum-Beat* (newspaper published for the Brooklyn fair), March 1, 1864, p. 4; March 2, 1864, p. 4; and March 3, 1864, p. 4.

8. *Harper's Weekly*, June 3, 1865, p. 339; *The Daily Morning Drum-Beat*, March 3, 1864, p. 4.

9. Ralph Waldo Emerson, "The President's Proclamation," *Atlantic Monthly*, X (November 1862), 639.

10. Richard Hofstadter, *The American Political Tradition and the Men Who Made It* (New York: Alfred A. Knopf, 1948), p. 132.

11. Karl Marx to Frederick Engels, Oct. 16, 1862, in Marx and Engels, *The Civil War in the United States* (N.Y.: Citadel, 1961) p. 258; Emerson, "The President's Proclamation," p. 639; Henry Greenleaf Pearson, *The Life of*

John A. Andrew (2 vols., Boston: Houghton Mifflin, 1904), II, 51; H. Draper Hunt, *Hannibal Hamlin of Maine: Lincoln's First Vice-President* (Syracuse, N.Y.: Syracuse University Press, 1969), p. 161; *New York Times* quoted in John Hope Franklin, *The Emancipation Proclamation* (Garden City, N.Y.: Doubleday, 1963), p. 62.

12. John Hay, "Life in the White House in the Time of Lincoln," *Century*, new ser., XIX (1890), 33.

13. Charles Oscar Paullin, "Hawthorne and Lincoln," *Americana*, IV (1909), 890–891; James R. Mellow, *Nathaniel Hawthorne and His Times* (Boston: Houghton Mifflin, 1980), p. 582.

14. Justin Kaplan, *Walt Whitman: A Life* (New York: Simon & Schuster, 1980), pp. 260, 271, 261.

15. Quoted in Rice, *Reminiscences of Abraham Lincoln*, p. 472.

16. David Lane, "A Soldier's Diary, 1862–1865" (1905), quoted in John W. Schildt, *Four Days in October* (Chewsville, Md.: 1978), pp. 18–19; John Nicolay, "Lincoln's Personal Appearance," *Century* (October 1891), 933.

17. The quotation is from the caption to the woodcut engraving, *c.* 1861, from the collection of Harold Holzer.

18. *Coll. Works of Lincoln*, IV, 385.

19. Winfred Porter Truesdell, *Catalog Raisonné of the Portraits of Col. Elmer E. Ellsworth* (Champlain, N.Y.: The Print Connoisseur, 1927).

20. Curtin quoted in *Carpenter's Great National Painting. President Lincoln's Emancipation Proclamation. . . . On Exhibition at the Gallery of Williams & Everett, 234 Washington St., Boston* (n.p., n.d.), p. 1.

21. Quoted in Roy P. Basler, *The Lincoln Legend: A Study in Changing Conceptions* (Boston: Houghton Mifflin, 1935), pp. 202–203, 179.

22. There would be three hundred photographers in New York City alone by the following census. See Pollack, *Picture History of Photography*, p. 224.

23. See Charles Eberstadt, *Lincoln's Emancipation Proclamation* (New York: Duschnes Crawford, 1950), pp. 39, 44.

24. Louis A. Warren, "Calligraphic Lincoln Portraits," *Lincoln Lore*, no. 626 (April 7, 1941); see also Harold Holzer, "Lincoln Calligraphy," *Lincoln Herald*, LXXXI (Winter 1979), 270–272.

25. Nicholas B. Wainwright, *Philadelphia in the Romantic Age of Lithography* (Philadelphia: Historical Society of Pennsylvania, 1958), p. 65; Marzio, *The Democratic Art*, p. 26.

26. *Old Print Gallery Showcase* (catalogue), III (July–August 1976), 77.

27. Carpenter, *Six Months at the White House*, pp. 157–158.

28. *Coll. Works of Lincoln*, IV, 240.

29. George C. Groce and David H. Wallace, *The New-York Historical Society's Dictionary of Artists in America, 1564–1860* (New Haven: Yale University Press, 1957), p. 422.

30. John W. Forney to Abraham Lincoln, December 30, 1862, Abraham Lincoln Papers, Library of Congress (microfilm).

31. *Coll. Works of Lincoln*, VI, 118, 125.

32. "Lincoln's Growth as Portraits Tell It," *New York Times Magazine*, February 7, 1932.

33. Whiting's pamphlet had convinced Lincoln that he had adequate constitutional power to issue the proclamation. The little work was important enough to be shown in Francis B. Carpenter's monumental painting celebrating the Emancipation Proclamation, which is discussed below. See Carpenter, *Six Months at the White House*, 353. Marchant's letter to Whiting of November 1, 1870, mentioning the other painting, is in the Concord Free Library, Concord, Massachusetts. The painter did not part with his copy painting of Lincoln until around 1870.

34. R. M. Deven, *American Progress: Or the Great Events of the Greatest Century* (Chicago: Hugh Heron, 1882), p. 546.

35. Carpenter, *Six Months at the White House*, pp. 10–11.

36. *Ibid.*, pp. 11–12.

37. *Ibid.*, pp. 25, 9.
38. *Ibid.*, pp. 12–13.
39. Francis B. Carpenter to Owen Lovejoy, January 5, 1864 (typed copy), Louis A. Warren Lincoln Library and Museum. Carpenter first went to Samuel Sinclair of the New York *Tribune* and asked him to introduce him to both Schuyler Colfax, an influential Republican congressman from Indiana, and Lovejoy. Lincoln had already consented to sittings by Christmas 1862. Charles Hamilton and Lloyd Ostendorf, *(Lincoln in Photographs: An Album of Every Known Pose* (Norman, Oklahoma: University of Oklahoma Press, 1963), p. 186.
40. Carpenter, *Six Months at the White House*, pp. 18, 19.
41. *Ibid.*, pp. 19, 20, 27–28.
42. *Ibid.*, p. 29.
43. Tyler Dennett, ed., *Lincoln and the Civil War in the Diaries and Letters of John Hay* (New York: Dodd, Mead, 1939), p. 197; Howard K. Beale, ed., *Diary of Gideon Welles* (3 vols., New York: W. W. Norton, 1960), I, 548–549.
44. *Diary of Gideon Welles*, I, 527; Carpenter, *Six Months at the White House*, p. 37.
45. *Six Months at the White House*, pp. 223, 30.
46. *Ibid.*, pp. 281, 39, 106–107, 30–31, 48–52, and 55.
47. *Ibid.*, p. 152; see also Francis B. Carpenter, "Anecdotes and Reminiscences of President Lincoln," in Henry J. Raymond, *Life and Public Services of Abraham Lincoln* (New York: Derby & Miller, 1865), p. 763. This Carpenter essay appeared as an appendix to Raymond's biography, one of the first published after Lincoln's death. Derby & Miller, the publishers, had also issued Ritchie's engraving of the Carpenter painting, through whom this "collaboration" was undoubtedly arranged. By the next year, Carpenter had expanded his article into a book—and placed it with another publisher.
48. Carpenter, *Six Months at the White House*, pp. 350–352.
49. Dennett, *Lincoln and the Civil War in the Diaries and Letters of John Hay*, p. 272; Carpenter, *Six Months at the White House*, p. 353; Carpenter, "Anecdotes," p. 764.
50. David McNeely Stauffer, *American Engravers upon Copper and Steel* (New York: Grolier Club, 1907), pp. 222–223; pamphlet issued by Williams & Everett Gallery; Turner and Turner, *Mary Todd Lincoln: Her Life and Letters*, p. 368. After the publication of Carpenter's book, Mrs. Lincoln grew very angry with the artist, for reasons that are unknown. See Turner and Turner, *Mary Todd Lincoln*, p. 464.
51. Architect of the Capitol's Accession Sheet; Charles Fairman, *Art & Artists of the U.S.A.* (Washington, D.C.: U.S. Government Printing Office, 1927), p. 305; R. Gerald McMurtry, "Carpenter's Painting: 'The First Reading . . .'", *Lincoln Lore*, no. 1482 (August 1961), and "Carpenter's Painting . . . Part II," *Lincoln Lore*, no. 1483 (September 1961).
52. See Harold Holzer, "Presidential Proximity: 'Musical Chairs' in Lincoln Emancipation Prints," *Lincoln Herald*, LXXX (Fall 1978), pp. 148–154; Francis B. Carpenter, *The Inner Life of Abraham Lincoln* (Boston: Houghton, Osgood, 1878), p. 209 and inside back cover with advertisement for Ritchie print.
53. George McCullough Anderson, *The Work of Adalbert Johann Volck* (Baltimore: privately printed, 1970), pp. vii–xi; *Adalbert Volck: Fifth Column Artist* (gallery notes for exhibition at the National Portrait Gallery, Smithsonian Institution, September 29, 1978–March 25, 1979).
54. Carpenter, *Six Months at the White House*, p. 262.
55. Mitgang, *Abraham Lincoln: A Press Portrait*, pp. 419, 417.
56. *Coll. Works of Lincoln*, VIII, 191–192.
57. *Ibid.*, VIII, 27; E. C. Middleton to Abraham Lincoln, August 12, 1864, Clark County Historical Society, Springfield, Ohio (photocopy in Louis A. Warren Lincoln Library and Museum).
58. Quoted in James R. Mellon, *The Face of Lincoln* (New York: Viking, 1979), p. 163.

59. Carpenter, *Six Months at the White House*, pp. 232–233.
60. Quoted in Kaplan, *Whitman*, p. 302.

Part III APOTHEOSIS AND APOCRYPHA

1. *Punch*, May 6, 1865, p. 182.
2. Basler, *The Lincoln Legend*, p. 164.
3. Louis M. Gottschalk, "Notes of a Pianist," in Kenneth A. Bernard, *Lincoln and the Music of the Civil War* (Caldwell, Idaho: Caxton Printers, 1966), p. 308.
4. *Coll. Works of Lincoln*, VIII, 333.
5. *Ibid.*, VIII, 399.
6. Basler, *The Lincoln Legend*, p. 165.
7. Lloyd Lewis, *Myths After Lincoln* (New York: Harcourt, Brace, 1929), pp. 95, 96.
8. *Ibid.*, pp. 81, 82, 109.
9. *Ibid.*, pp. 111, 112, 108, 109, 115; Thomas Reed Turner, *Beware the People Weeping: Public Opinion and the Assassination of Abraham Lincoln* (Baton Rouge, La.: Louisiana State University Press, 1982), pp. 87–88.
10. Hess and Kaplan, *The Ungentlemanly Art*, pp. 90–91.
11. P. J. Staudenraus, *Mr. Lincoln's Washington* (New York: Thomas Yoseloff, 1967), p. 454; Matthew Simpson, *Funeral Address Delivered at the Burial of President Lincoln . . . May 4, 1865* (New York: Carlton & Porter, 1865), p. 5; Theodore Calvin Pease and James G. Randall, eds., *The Diary of Orville Hickman Browning* (2 vols., Springfield, Ill.: Illinois State Historical Library, 1933), II, 22; Lewis, *Myths After Lincoln*, p. 404.
12. Bernard, *Lincoln and the Music of the Civil War*, p. 308; Oldroyd, *Lincoln Memorial*, p. 251.
13. David T. Valentine, ed., *Obsequies of Abraham Lincoln in the City of New York . . .* (New York: Edmund Jones & Co., 1866), p. 199.
14. *Ibid.*, pp. 56, 57.
15. *Ibid.*, pp. 66–67.
16. *Ibid.*, pp. 61, 62, 74, 69, 87.
17. *Ibid.*, pp. 78, 77.
18. *Ibid.*, pp. 80, 81, 85, 87, 60.
19. *Harper's Weekly*, July 15, 1865, p. 438.
20. Wick, *George Washington*, p. 66.
21. *Diary of Orville Hickman Browning*, II, 22.
22. Alexander Hay Ritchie's engraving, *Death of President Lincoln*, claimed to represent the persons actually present and had eleven letters of endorsement from persons who claimed to be present at Lincoln's deathbed, but the engraving showed twenty-four people in the little room. *Ritchie's Historical Picture, Death of President Lincoln . . .* (New York: A. H. Ritchie, 1868), pp. 5–11.
23. Nancy F. Cott, *The Bonds of Womanhood: "Women's Sphere" in New England, 1780–1835* (New Haven: Yale University Press, 1977), p. 64 (punctuation added).
24. Benjamin P. Thomas, *Abraham Lincoln: A Biography* (New York: Alfred A. Knopf, 1952), p. 464.
25. Turner and Turner, *Mary Todd Lincoln: Her Life and Letters*, p. 187.
26. Elizabeth Keckley, *Behind the Scenes* (New York: G. W. Carleton, 1868), pp. 104–105.
27. Turner and Turner, *Mary Todd Lincoln: Her Life and Letters*, p. 285.
28. John S. Goff, *Robert Todd Lincoln: A Man in His Own Right* (Norman, Okla.: University of Oklahoma Press, 1969), pp. 46–48.
29. *Lincoln and His Family* (advertising brochure) (Rochester, N.Y.: R. H. Curran n.d.).
30. *Coll. Works of Lincoln*, IV, 195.
31. Horace Bushnell, *Christian Nurture* (orig. pub. 1861; New Haven, Conn.: Yale University Press, 1967).
32. Hamilton and Ostendorf, *Lincoln in Photographs*, pp. 172–183; Carpenter, *Six Months at the White House*, p. 35.
33. Turner and Turner, *Mary Todd Lincoln*, pp. 283–285.

34. *Ibid.*, pp. 285, 298.

35. Van Deren Coke, *The Painter and the Photograph: From Delacroix to Warhol* (Albuquerque, N.M.: University of New Mexico Press, 1964), p. 28.

36. Stauffer, *American Engravers upon Copper and Steel*, pp. 38–39. George H. Smyser, "The Lincoln Family in 1861: A History of the Painting and the Engraving," *Journal of the Illinois State Historical Society*, XXII (July 1929), p. 358.

37. William R. Taylor, *Cavalier and Yankee: The Old South and American National Character* (orig. pub. 1961; Garden City, N.Y.: Doubleday, 1963), pp. 93–94.

38. Quoted in Wainwright, *Philadelphia in the Romantic Age of Lithography*, pp. 42, 45; Marzio, *The Democratic Art*, pp. 128, 117.

39. Walter E. Houghton, *The Victorian Frame of Mind, 1830–1870* (New Haven: Yale University Press, 1957), pp. 343–344; Turner and Turner, *Mary Todd Lincoln*, p. 189.

40. Wick, *George Washington*, p. 122; *Lincoln and His Family* (advertising brochure).

41. Edward Waldo Emerson and Waldo Emerson Forbes, eds., *Journals of Ralph Waldo Emerson* (10 vols., Boston: Houghton Mifflin, 1909–14), VIII, 300.

42. Wick, *George Washington*, pp. 7–8, and Lillian B. Miller in *ibid.*, p. xiii. Cf. Peter Karsten, *Patriot-Heroes in England and America: Political Symbolism and Changing Values over Three Centuries* (Madison, Wis.: University of Wisconsin Press, 1978), p. 89.

43. Roy P. Basler, ed., *The Collected Works of Abraham Lincoln: Supplement, 1832–1865* (Westport, Conn.: Greenwood, 1974), 55; *Coll. Works of Lincoln*. IV, 190.

44. Two days later, Lincoln repeated the same thought but in a more characteristically humble manner: "I cannot but know what you all know, that, without a name, perhaps without a reason why I should have a name, there has fallen upon me a task such as did not rest even upon the Father of his country. . . ." *Coll. Works of Lincoln*, IV, 204.

45. See, for example, George B. Forgie, *Patricide in the House Divided; A Psychological Interpretation of Lincoln and His Age* (New York: W. W. Norton, 1979), pp. 68–69.

46. *Coll. Works of Lincoln*, I. 279.

47. *Ibid.*, II, 378; III, 550; I, 170, 172–173, 312, 333, 502.

48. Harold Holzer, "Lincoln and Washington: The Printmakers Blessed Their Union," *Register of the Kentucky Historical Society*, LXXV (July 1977), 204–213.

49. Louis A. Warren, "Nancy Hanks' Birthplace," *Lincoln Lore*, no. 28 (October 1929).

50. Phoebe Lloyd Jacobs, "John James Barralet and the Apotheosis of George Washington," *Winterthur Portfolio*, 12 (Charlottesville, Va.: University Press of Virginia, 1977), pp. 115–137. The following discussion is indebted above all to Jacobs, but also to Davida Tennenbaum Deutsch, "Washington Memorial Prints," *Antiques*, III (February 1977), 329–331; Patricia A. Anderson, *Promoted to Glory: The Apotheosis of George Washington* (Northampton, Mass.: Smith College Museum of Art, 1980); Wick, *George Washington, passim.*; and Anita Schorsch, "Mourning Art: A Neoclassical Reflection in America," *American Art Journal*, VIII (May 1976), 11–15.

51. Wick, *George Washington*, p. 166.

52. *Ibid.*

53. The term *rudis* was also used for Liberty's staff, and it referred to the rod given to the freed gladiator after his term was served. John Edwin Sandys, *A Companion to Latin Studies* (Cambridge, England: Cambridge University Press, 1929), pp. 306–307.

54. Morse was forced to accept another two-volume set, Carl Schurz's *Henry Clay*, because Schurz threatened to publish it at the same time any other volume on Clay appeared in the "American Statesman" series. Arthur Schlesinger, Jr., "General Introudction," in Albert

Bushnell Hart, *Salmon P. Chase* (New York: Chelsea House, 1981), pp. xii–xiii.

55. Carleton Putnam, *Theodore Roosevelt,* Volume 1: *The Formative Years, 1858–1886* (New York: Charles Scribner's Sons, 1958), p. 479; *Washington Post,* February 21, 1983.

56. P. M. Zall, ed., *Abe Lincoln Laughing* (Berkeley: University of California Press, 1982), p. 122.

57. Wilson, *Intimate Memories,* p. 419.

58. Stefan Lorant, *Lincoln: A Picture Story of His Life,* rev. ed. (New York: W. W. Norton, 1969), pp. 304–307; Milton Kaplan, "Heads of States," in *Winterthur Portfolio,* 6 (Charlottesville, Va.: University Press of Virginia, 1970), pp. 135–150.

59. Hamilton and Ostendorf, *Lincoln in Photographs,* pp. 390–392.

60. John Hay, "Life in the White House in the Time of Lincoln," p. 37.

61. Quoted in William E. Barton, *Abraham Lincoln and Walt Whitman* (Indianapolis: Bobbs-Merrill, 1928), p. 181.

62. See Fig. 76.

63. Louis A. Warren, "Littlefield's Engraving of Lincoln," *Lincoln Lore,* no. 592 (August 12, 1940), John H. Littlefield, autograph "Statement," Oct. 8, 1875, in New-York Historical Society.

64. Groce and Wallace, *Dictionary of Artists in America,* p. 279.

65. Allen E. Kent, "Early Commercial Lithography in Wisconsin," *Wisconsin Magazine of History,* XXXVI (Summer 1953), 249.

66. Groce and Wallace, *Dictionary of Artists in America,* p. 424; *Catalogue of American Portraits in the New-York Historical Society* (2 vols., New Haven: Yale University Press, 1974), I, 630; John Lobb, ed., *The Life and Times of Frederick Douglass . . .* (London: Christian Age, 1882), p. 325.

67. Louis A. Warren, "Marshall's Engraving of Lincoln," *Lincoln Lore,* no. 591 (August 5, 1940); *Announcement: Marshall's Portrait of Lincoln* (advertising brochure) (New York: Ticknor & Fields, 1866).

68. *Sotheby's Printed and Manuscript Americana,* (catalogue), June 22, 1941, item 231. Carpenter conveniently ignored his own reliance on photographs for his "life" portraits.

69. Quoted in Basler, *The Lincoln Legend,* p. 283.

70. Charles R. Cushman, *Memorial Addresses Delivered Before the Two Houses of Congress* (Washington, D.C.: U.S. Government Printing Office, 1903), Appendix, p. 96.

INDEX

quality of artwork: in *The Assassination,* *151;* in Baker's print, *54;* in Carpenter's painting, 179; in Hart's print, *163;* in Hohenstein's print, *182;* in Lincoln/Tad print, *172;* in Magee's print, *156;* in prints, generally, 20, 43, 183–84; in prints following Emancipation Proclamation, 102; in Rosenthal's print, *155;* in Sartain's print, 171–74; in Wiest's print, *178;* in Wigwam print, *13,* 14. *See also* accuracy of scene depicted

racism, in cartoons, *37, 38, 39, 40, 43*
railsplitter image, 6, 15–16; in cartoons, *37, 38, 40;* in display of prints, *32,* 73; in prints, 16, *36, 105;* on sheet music cover, *35;* in verse, 78, 148
Read, John Meredith, 58
Rease, William H., print by, *36*
Republican National Convention of 1860, 9–14
Richmond, Virginia *Dispatch,* 135
Ritchie, Alexander Hay: and pirating of print by, *125;* print by, 122–24, *123,* 126
Roosevelt, Franklin Delano, 203
Roosevelt, Theodore, 203
Rosenthal, L. N., print by, *155*
Rosenthal, Max, print by, *155*
Ross, A. M., 140
Russell, Benjamin B., print by, *93*
Russell, Gilman R., print by, *101*

Sadd, Henry S.: print by, *68;* and print based on Sadd print, *69*
sales of artwork, 80–84
"sanitary fairs," 83–84
Sartain, Henry, print by, *109*
Sartain, John: prints by, *108,* 110, 197, *197, 207;* print of, *109*
Sartain, Samuel, print by, 65–66, *65*
Sartain, William, print by, *160,* 171
Schaus, W., print by, *49,* 50
Scott, Winfield, 91, *93*
Scripps, John Locke, 18
Sealy, A., print by, *31*
second campaign: *Abraham Lincoln, 131; Grand, National Union, 130. See also* cartoons, second campaign
Second Inaugural Address, 151, 153
sentimentalism in prints, 132, 165–67, 180, 184–87
Seward, William, H., 118–20; depicted in prints, *69, 101, 110, 123, 125, 191, 192*
Shakespearean themes: in cartoons, 132, *133;* in *The Martyr,* 153
sheet music: after assassination, 162–63; *Honest Old Abe,* 24; *Lincoln Quick step, 35;* and use in campaigns, 24, *24*
Sheridan, Philip, *134*
Sherman, William T., *134*
Sinclair, Thomas S., sheet music by, *35*
slavery: in cartoon, *41;* in prints, 85, *96, 96, 102, 195*
smiling, by Lincoln, in cartoon, *41*
Smith, Caleb B., *110, 123, 125*
Smith, John, print by, *172*

Smith, William, prints by, *178, 200*
Smithsonian Institution. *See* National Portrait Gallery, Smithsonian Institution
Stanton, Edwin M., 214; depicted in prints, *110, 123, 125, 155*
Stephens, Alexander H., *85*
Storey, Alfred & Co., print by, *185*
Strobridge, Hines, print by, 138
Strong, Thomas W., print by, *133*
Sumner, Charles, 214
Swander, R. Morris, *96*

Taylor, Tom, 148
Tazewell County Republican, 34
Ten Bears, *88*
Thomas, George, *134*
Ticknor & Fields, print by, *212*

ugliness, of Lincoln. *See* homeliness of Lincoln
Union, preservation of: *Grand, National Union, 130; Union, 69; The Union Must And Shall Be, 36*
Union League Club. *See* Art Collection of The Union League of Philadelphia
United States Capitol, painting in collection, *110,* 112
United States Sanitary Commission, 83–85
unknown printmakers, prints by, *43, 69, 151, 153, 172, 186, 192*